THE
BACKWARDS
HAND

THE BACKWARDS HAND

MATT LEE

A MEMOIR

Curbstone Books / Northwestern University Press
Evanston, Illinois

Curbstone Books
Northwestern University Press
www.nupress.northwestern.edu

Printed in the United States of America

10   9   8   7   6   5   4   3   2   1

Library of Congress Cataloging-in-Publication Data

Names: Lee, Matt, 1990– author.
Title: The backwards hand : a memoir / Matt Lee.
Description: Evanston : Curbstone Books/Northwestern University
    Press, 2024.
Identifiers: LCCN 2023053650 | ISBN 9780810147157 (paperback) |
    ISBN 9780810147164 (ebook)
Subjects: LCSH: Lee, Matt, 1990– | People with disabilities—United
    States—Biography. | People with disabilities—Social conditions. |
    Monsters—History.
Classification: LCC HV3013.L44 A3 2024 | DDC 305.908092—dc23/
    eng/20231116
LC record available at https://lccn.loc.gov/2023053650

For Umberto

Thou know'st how lame a cripple this world is.

—JOHN DONNE

CONTENTS

I came out wrong.

I

THE CREATURE WALKS AMONG US

The year is 1990. On July 26, President George H. W. Bush signs into law the landmark Americans with Disabilities Act. The day is warm but not too hot. The pristine green South Lawn of the White House is blanketed with smiling cripples. The ones who can clap do. Flanked by two activists in wheelchairs, Bush declares in his fake Texan accent, *Let the shameful wall of exclusion finally come tumbling down.*

Four days later, I am born at a hospital in central Maryland. I enter the world wet and bloody and screaming. The doctor congratulates my mother and father, the proud parents of what seems like a perfectly healthy baby boy.

Three days later, Saddam Hussein invades Kuwait. I cannot yet comprehend the news footage on every television— tanks rolling through the desert, oil refineries ablaze, the royal palace looted. And so the Gulf War begins.

Three months later, the film *Jacob's Ladder* is released. A bespectacled Tim Robbins plays a Vietnam vet plagued by bizarre hallucinations. During the climax, he is abducted and taken to a dilapidated hospital. Two men in white scrubs strap him to a gurney and wheel him through a series of increasingly nightmarish corridors. We see madmen in straitjackets, gnarled amputees, piles of bloody viscera on the cracked tile floor. In the operating chamber a surgeon with no eyes plunges a hypodermic needle into Robbins's forehead. We learn the awful truth. Our hero has been dead the whole time.

Right now, while writing this, I am thinking about how a doctor sitting in a cold, brown room behind a big black desk told me there is a high probability I will develop severe arthritis in my hands as I grow older—eventually, I will not be able to write at all.

There is no consensus on what constitutes disability. Still, the disabled population accounts for the single largest minority group in the United States, if not the world. Disability is the great equalizer. It is a community that does not discriminate, does not see color, gender, or class. Anyone can join, at any time.

The carnival barker addresses the crowd: *We didn't lie to you, folks. We told you we had living, breathing monstrosities. You laughed at them, shuddered at them, and yet, but for the accident of birth, you might be even as they are. They did not ask to be brought into the world. But into the world they came. Their code is a law unto themselves—offend one and you offend them all.*

In horror films, the killer is almost always disfigured in some outward fashion. Freddy Krueger, Jason Voorhees, Leatherface—all suffer from physical deformity. They were once men; now they are monsters.

My mother says nobody knew until I was a toddler. I have learned how to walk. My Nona crouches before me, auburn perm immaculate, costume jewelry jangling. She offers a chocolate peanut-butter cup, beckoning me with the treat. *Hold out your hand, my little apple.* I can only claw. *No, Matthew, like this!* And she demonstrates what I am supposed to do, show my palm. I want to tell her I cannot do as she asks. I have not yet learned the right words. When she tries to turn my hand herself, I cry out in pain.

The philosopher Julia Kristeva describes abjection as ambiguous, composite, in-between, like an apparition that lingers, a friend who stabs you in the back. Abjection is an uncanny terror that disrupts the fabric of our being. Cadavers, sewage, cripples, monstrosities—these are its trigger.

The ancient Greeks held a utilitarian view toward disability. Newborns were inspected for any signs of weakness. Those with obvious deformities were, according to Plutarch, thrown into a deep chasm or left outside to die of exposure. This practice was considered justified on the grounds that the children could offer no contributions to society and would therefore be a burden on the state. Aristotle suggested, *Let there be a law that no deformed child shall live.*

My wife and I want children. When we first got together, nearly a decade before we were married, having kids was out of the question. Neither of us desired to procreate. We grew older. We changed our minds. I worry how I will hold the delicate infant, support the paper-thin head, cradle the diaper-swelled bottom.

The monster is not without affection. Often he is a devoted family man, like Leatherface. Or a mama's boy, like Jason Voorhees. Or a doting father, like Freddy Krueger.

August 21, 1962. Tsutomu Miyazaki is born prematurely in Tokyo, weighing less than five pounds. The joints in his hands are fused together. He survives infancy but is forever unable to bend his wrists. Little Tsutomu, born a cripple, destined to become a monster.

My parents bring me to a pediatrician. He is impressed. *Now this is a rare case. I've only ever read about it. And here you are in the flesh!* The giant in a starchy white coat studies my pudgy little arms. The room is all soft, inoffensive pastels, with stuffed animals and lollipops at the ready to appease any wailing tykes who try to squirm away from the spikes and hammers and binds. He tells my parents I have a congenital birth defect called bilateral radioulnar synostosis. He explains how the bones in my forearms are fused. My hands will never turn—they are fixed. Permanent. I hear for the first time what will become a familiar refrain: *I'm sorry. He will have to live like this. There's nothing we can do.*

Defect from the Latin *defectus*, "failure," "absence," "weakness," "revolt."

My favorite game to play with Dad is the Claw. He throws me on the futon. I try to scurry away. He pins me down. Here comes the Claw—Dad's arm outstretched, fingers curled. He says, *No one escapes . . . the Claw!* He tickles me all over, and I scream with laughter and kick the mattress and finally wrestle free. He tucks me in, but I'm too wound up for bedtime. I stay awake reading comic books. Dad goes down into the basement. He calls it the Cave. He stays awake late like me, but I don't know what he does. I know he doesn't sleep in the same bed as Mom anymore.

Bruegel's *The Beggars* is an oil painting from 1568 housed at the Louvre. The scene shows five men and an old woman gathered in a courtyard, preparing for another day's panhandling. The gawping cripples wear carnivalesque headgear meant to represent different classes—cardboard crown for the king, paper shako for the army, beret for the bourgeoisie, cap for the peasantry, bishop's miter for the church. They are adorned in foxtails and carry crutches. The work is often cited as difficult, an enigma resisting interpretation. On the back of the wood canvas a previous owner wrote an inscription in Flemish: *Cripples, take heart, and may your affairs prosper.*

Always, the suspicion we are faking it, a long con to receive Social Security benefits we do not deserve. Nothing but a bunch of good-for-nothing freeloaders, lazy parasites sucking the blood from society's teat.

The actress Lupita Nyong'o was criticized for negatively portraying a character with spasmodic dysphonia, a condition that constricts the vocal cords, causing strained, disrupted speech. In the 2019 film *Us*, Nyong'o plays two characters—well-to-do mother Adelaide Wilson and her evil doppelgänger, Red. The decision to have the menacing Red suffer this speech impediment caused backlash to the point that Nyong'o publicly apologized on national television. Imagine, a Black woman chastised for demonizing a marginalized community.

The Civil Rights Act of 1964 prohibits discrimination based on race, color, religion, sex, or national origin. Cripples did not receive similar legal protections for another twenty-six years.

Kristeva warns that you cannot identify with the abject. At the same time, abjection is inextricable from our existence. Abjection— all that is foul, putrid, vulgar—is essential to life. Split open your stomach, crack your skull, cut your throat, and abjection spills out.

What does it mean to be abject, to be repellent, to be wrong? Should I define disability through those terms? Is someone with HIV disabled? What about alcoholics? Werewolves?

When I am old enough for school, my mother pulls the blue-eyed, blonde teacher aside and explains my condition. In class the other kids ask why I hold my crayons funny. The teacher announces, *Matthew is special.* I learn what it means to be patronized. I am special but not in a good way.

How old were you when you first stumbled across the invisible boundary separating normal from other? Man from monster?

Diane Arbus is known for her stark black-and-white photographs. Her subjects are often outcasts—transgender people, mental patients, sideshow performers. Arbus remains a controversial figure, and critics have long decried her work as exploitative. During the 1967 group exhibition *New Documents* at the Museum of Modern Art in New York, a young man spat on one of Arbus's prints. Her unflinching portraits of disabled individuals have been met with particular disgust. A dwarf lounging in his hotel room. A giant stooped inside his parents' apartment. A woman in a wheelchair wearing a grotesque mask.

The monster often hides behind a mask. This is only a temporary salve. The costume can be shed, the deformity cannot. To mend the monster's aberrations would require a miracle.

The Gospel of John recounts a meeting between Jesus and a cripple near the Sheep Gate in Jerusalem. For thirty-eight years, the man had lain paralyzed on a mat beside a magical pool called Bethesda, the waters of which could cure disease. Jesus asked the man, *Do you want to be made well?* The cripple told Jesus he could not reach Bethesda because he had no one to help him. Jesus instructed, *Arise, take up your mat, and walk.* The cripple was cured instantly. Jesus left him with a warning: *Sin no more, so that nothing worse happens to you.*

My hands appear askew when clasped in prayer.

Numerous religious organizations opposed the Americans with Disabilities Act of 1990, citing concerns over undue financial strain that would result from making churches handicap accessible. Apparently, God wanted to know who was planning on paying for all those wheelchair ramps.

I am taken to receive my first communion when I turn seven. St. John's is a looming white, stone church with a big sign out front—Pray to End Abortion. My mother and father and little sister watch from the pews. I walk to the altar wearing my Sunday best. Too-big black slacks, stiff white button-up, polyester vest. The organ pipes moaning, holy incense stinging my eyes, the ancient priest in his gilded robe prepares the sacrament. Unable to cup my hands, I stick out my tongue to receive the body of Christ. I beg forgiveness for my sins. The Lord does not heal me.

Leviticus 21:17–20—*None of your offspring throughout their generations who has a defect may approach to offer the bread of his God. For whatever man he is that has a defect, he shall not draw near: a blind man, or a lame, or he who has a flat nose, or any deformity, or a man who has an injured foot, or an injured hand, or hunchbacked, or a dwarf, or one who has a defect in his eye, or an itching disease, or scabs, or who has damaged testicles.*

Lon Chaney became a massive star after his performance as Quasimodo in the 1923 film *The Hunchback of Notre Dame.* Chaney based his faithful depiction on the Victor Hugo source material. Quasimodo is one-eyed. He has gone deaf from the cathedral's clanging bells. His face is misshapen and his body covered with thick patches of wiry hair. The makeup Chaney used permanently damaged his vision. After shooting wrapped, the actor wore glasses for the rest of his life.

In the Bible, visual impairment is considered among the lowest degradations.

As a child, I hate the way people look at me when I take change, carry a plate, shake hands. At school, I dread clapping games. Whenever the teacher tells us to sit crisscross-applesauce on the puke-green carpet, my chest constricts. Patty-cake, Quack Diddly Oso, Concentration

64, Miss Mary Mack—my hands were not made for these diversions. Nobody wants to be my partner. I can clap by myself but not the same way the other kids can.

Tsutomu is also an unhappy child. His younger sisters mock his funny hands. His classmates are worse. He becomes a perennial loner, escaping into comic books, horror movies. In family photos he never shows his hands. His eyes are often closed.

Pity the monster. Beneath the monster's ugliness lies a soul, humanity masked by deformity. Within the monster we all see ourselves, what we might become.

Sometimes monstrosity is inherited. I tell my wife there is a chance our child will be born with my same affliction. A Punnett square shows the odds: 50-50.

One of Arbus's most famous photographs is from 1970, *A Jewish giant at home with his parents, in the Bronx, N.Y.* The giant is Eddie Carmel, who experienced sudden and massive growth from an inoperable tumor that had sprouted on his pituitary gland. Arbus first met Carmel at a Ringling Brothers circus. When she photographed him years later in his parents' living room, Carmel had retired from performing and was forced to walk with two canes.

In the photo, both parents stare up at their son, a colossus plucked from some fairy-tale book and transplanted to their modest apartment.

Arbus says reality becomes fantastic if we scrutinize it closely enough. Like the way people marvel when I explain my condition, as if unable to imagine what my hands cannot do. Then come the questions, the prodding. The bold ones test my wrists themselves. Next, the look of shock, bewilderment. They do not believe in my storybook curse. They think I am trying to fool them. They need to feel the immovable flesh.

Bilateral, "affecting two sides." *Radioulnar,* "of two bones in a human forearm, the radius and ulna." *Synostosis,* "the fusion of adjacent bones."

There are two distinct branches in disability studies, essentialism and constructivism. Essentialists regard disability as inherent to the person, a biological or psychological phenomenon, a medical condition. Constructivists view disability as a purely social construct: some argue that disability does not exist at all, others claim everyone is disabled.

Two branches. Two bones. Two hands.

Dad brings me to New York City with his girlfriend and her four daughters. The girlfriend's husband has a lot of money. We stay at the Plaza Hotel in a big, glitzy suite. On the first night, Dad takes us out to a steak house. He orders filet mignon and scotch. The drink looks delicious, like caramel. I have ginger ale. Dad asks for another round. The girlfriend's daughters keep whining. They smell of stale urine. I breathe through my mouth. Another round. Dad's face is red. He won't shut up. The girlfriend pays the bill. Back at the hotel, the usual routine. The girlfriend screaming and screaming and Dad screaming back. The girlfriend flings a thick glass tumbler at Dad's head. He ducks, and the glass shatters against the cream-colored wall. I hide in the bathtub with the four daughters. I breathe through my mouth. Security comes. They set up a folding cot for Dad. The girlfriend puts us all in bed with her. The next morning we go to Rockefeller Center. Dad wants to be on *The Today Show*. No one mentions the scotch, the broken glass, the security guards. We stand at the front of the crowd pressed against the guardrail. The cameraman pans our way. We wave. And scream and scream.

Tod Browning's 1932 film *Freaks* features a largely disabled cast, many of whom he scouted from circuses and sideshows. Contrary to popular attitudes of the time, the "freaks" in the film are depicted as self-reliant. Prince Randian, the Living Torso, rolls and lights his own cigarettes sans appendages. The Siamese Twins both have their own lovers. The Human Skeleton is married to the Bearded Lady, who gives birth to a baby girl. The Armless Wonder clenches a dagger between his teeth as he squirms through the mud, ready to slice up the treacherous strongman Hercules. Remember the code of the freaks: *Offend one and you offend them all.*

I learn to avoid playing sports. A simple game of catch proves comically challenging. My hands seem designed to repel whatever is thrown my way. When we play flag football at recess, I am always picked last. On the schoolyard blacktop, I climb up the geodesic dome and observe. Jeffrey wants to play four square. Colin, the tallest kid in fifth grade, laughs at him like a dolphin: *Get fucked, retard.* For a ten-year-old he has a sophisticated vocabulary. I stay perched. Jeffrey's in the special ed class. His speech is slurred, slow, like his mind. At the insult, Jeffrey rages. Colin is bleeding on the asphalt by the time Miss Kelly intervenes.

What the monster lacks in beauty he makes up for with brute force. Jason Voorhees may have been born with hydrocephalus, a swelling of the head caused by excessive buildup of cerebrospinal fluid, but he also possesses superhuman strength. Jason has claimed nearly 150 victims over the course of a dozen films, including a boy in a wheelchair who takes a machete to the face before tumbling down a flight of stairs—freeze-frame.

Supercrips are disabled people who defy their physical limitations to perform extraordinary acts. The blind man who scales Mount Everest. The amputee who runs marathons on prosthetic limbs. The cripple becomes a source of inspiration rather than an object of pity or fear.

At school, my friends exchange swear words at lunch. I learn a lot. Tobin blows bubbles in his carton of chocolate milk and picks at his mullet. He asks me the worst word I know. *Shithead,* I tell him. He peels the cheese off his slice of pizza and slurps down the mangled strands: *That's nothing. My brother called me a cocksucker. And a motherfucker.* I laugh but don't repeat the words. Tobin continues: *Know what I did? I gave him the finger. You know what the middle finger means? Fuck you!* He demonstrates: *Try it.* I look at my lunch tray and poke around the gluey mashed potatoes with a plastic fork. *I can't.* Tobin calls me a chicken. I tell him it's because of my hands. Tobin cackles, his lips shiny with grease. *Matt can't flick people off! He can't flip the bird!* In my head, I call Tobin all the new words I've learned.

Kristeva tells us abjection is a paradox. Unknowable, beyond desire, a violent and painful joy. The same joy I take from watching limbs hacked off, skulls split open, abdomens disemboweled in horror movies. All pretend, of course, but the makeup can be rather convincing.

Arbus says photographs are like a stain, proof of what once was, maddeningly still. Even when you look away, the photograph remains, waiting for you. Like my class photos from every year at school, in which I sometimes smile and always hide my hands.

My mother plays the Wicked Witch of the West. For the performance, she puts on a black cloak and pointy hat. She glues fake sharp nails to her fingers, attaches a long rubber nose, paints her face green. I know she is my mother, but she is something else too, and seeing her transformed, I love her and fear her at the same time. I become obsessed with *The Wizard of Oz*, watching and rewinding the tape so frequently that the spool snaps. I like the scary parts best. The demonic flying monkeys, the spear-wielding Winkies, the Wicked Witch astride her broomstick.

In Theravada Buddhism, disability places one at a lower level of enlightenment, a result of bad karma from a past life. As in Christianity, deformities are divine punishment, spiritual disability: cripples must suffer to build better karma for the next life.

What sin did I commit in my past life? What did I do to deserve this?

During the eugenics movement of the early twentieth century, American doctors called for disabled persons to be involuntarily sterilized lest they further taint the gene pool.

II

THE DISEMBODIED

The end of the millennium signals the conclusion of my parents' marriage. I do not handle it well. I distract myself with comics and cartoons, books and movies. I start writing stories in a notebook at night. I take acting lessons and audition for local stage productions. My mother's family are all artists. We take trips to New York City to see my aunts and uncles perform on Broadway. My mother's twin sister has a children's theater company where we live, in Frederick, Maryland. She casts me as Tiny Tim in *A Christmas Carol*, my first time playing a cripple. I hobble onto the stage with my crutch, wearing my Dickensian peasant clothes. *God bless us, every one!*

Like a role the actor takes on, the abject permeates you. You become abject.

One of us, one of us. Gooble gobble, gooble gobble.

Several figures in Diego Velázquez's painting *Las Meninas* meet our gaze, including the artist himself. Beside Infanta

Margaret Theresa stand the German Maria Bárbola and the Italian Nicolas Pertusato, both of whom were court dwarfs of the king and queen of Spain. Unusually for the seventeenth century, the two dwarfs are depicted with dignity, Bárbola standing proud, staring thoughtfully back at the viewer. After Philip V's reorganization of the royal infrastructure, the position of court dwarf was eliminated, deemed antiquated, out of fashion, barbaric. The dwarfs were deported to their home countries.

For decades, a myth has persisted that one of the Munchkins can be seen hanging himself in the background of *The Wizard of Oz.* Though long debunked (it is a bird, not a dwarf), numerous articles and videos online purport having evidence to the contrary. The actor, so the story goes, was distraught by poor working conditions on set, which drove him to commit suicide.

Susan Sontag famously attacked Diane Arbus in her essay "Freak Show." She accused Arbus of being a voyeur, a cynic, a wealthy white woman fraternizing with the Other for kicks. Sontag was repulsed by Arbus's grotesque subjects, too ugly to be art. For Sontag, there is no majesty in a photograph of dwarfs—there are only dwarfs.

Most people are afraid of cripples like me because they do not know how to act around us. Would you treat me as normal? Pretend nothing is wrong? Would you coddle me, infantilize me? Do you pity me? Fear me?

When *Freaks* was released in 1932, critics panned it: *Anyone who considers this entertainment should be placed in the pathological ward in some hospital.* And: *There is no excuse for this picture. It took a weak mind to produce it and it takes a strong stomach to look at it.*

I make new friends at school. A rattailed country boy, a hyperactive Mexican immigrant who can run a five-minute mile, and the tallest kid in our class. They roast me for not being able to go *high five, down low, too slow.* They start calling me Retard Arms. We laugh together, and I understand what it means to be a joke.

What do you call a guy with no arms and no legs when he's waiting at the door? Matt!

Tod Browning and Lon Chaney collaborated on the 1927 film *The Unknown*, a silent-era precursor to *Freaks*. Chaney plays Alonzo the Armless, a circus performer who uses his feet to throw knives at his beautiful partner Nanon—a young Joan Crawford. Alonzo has two secrets. He is desperately in love with Nanon. He is also an impostor, a fugitive pretending to be armless as a gimmick for his act. Nanon has a phobia of arms and refuses to let men grope her. Naturally, she dotes on the seemingly armless Alonzo. To win Nanon's affections, Alonzo convinces a doctor to amputate his arms. He is finished pretending. He has become a true freak. But the persistence of the strongman Malabar has made Nanon conquer her fear of arms. When Malabar and Nanon announce their plans to be married, Alonzo bursts into hysterical laughter that devolves into anguished sobs.

Kristeva says abjection implores and atomizes us in equal measure.

Alonzo plots to kill his rival. He sabotages a stunt rigged to look as if Malabar were holding two galloping horses steady with ropes tied to his biceps. If Alonzo succeeds, the illusion will become a reality, and the strongman's arms will be ripped off. When Nanon runs to subdue the horses, Alonzo pushes her from danger and is himself trampled to death. The penultimate title card reads: *So . . . for Alonzo there was an end to Hate called Death . . . and for Nanon, an end to Hate . . . called Love.*

Tsutomu watches too many movies. He falls behind and graduates from high school at the bottom of his class. He wants to be an English teacher, but no university will have him. He finds work at a print shop and lives with his parents. He shares a room with his sister. He has no prospects and no friends, but he does have dreams, unspeakable fantasies, of what he might become, what he might accomplish.

Shortly after the release of his first novel, the American writer Hob Broun underwent spinal surgery. Initially planning to remove what they thought was a cyst, doctors discovered a large tumor. The operation was a success in that Broun survived, but he was left paralyzed, bound to a respirator. He could no longer breathe for himself, let alone hold a pencil.

People I know have told me they attempted to go a day without turning their hands and found it utterly impossible. They cannot help themselves. Neither can I.

Quasimodo with a dagger in his back, watching the woman he desires embrace another man—a handsome, normal man. Quasimodo bleeds out, brokenhearted, ringing his own death toll. The grand bell at Notre Dame swings silently above his corpse.

My father stops paying child support. He has a new family to provide for. My mother takes a graphic design job fifty miles east in Baltimore. She works long hours. Most days I do not see her until nightfall. My sister and I are shuffled between babysitters. There are aunts and uncles, grand-parents and old family friends, after-school clubs and play rehearsals, therapy sessions.

During the Dark Ages, there existed a widespread belief that cripples were closer to heaven because they had expe-rienced purgatory on earth.

Arbus says the freak has a quality of legend, like a charac-ter from a fairy tale who demands an answer to a riddle. Freaks, she explains, are true aristocrats. Unlike normal people, freaks do not live their lives dreading what misfor-tune may befall them. Freaks are born with their tragedy.

During test screenings for *Freaks*, one woman threatened to sue MGM after claiming the film caused her to have a miscarriage. In the original ending, the villainous trapeze artist Cleopatra is mutilated beneath a tree, and her lover, Hercules, is brutally castrated. This footage was cut by censors and is now considered lost.

Pop, my father's father, watches me when Mom works late. I sit in the menthol secondhand smoke of his condo, absorbing the wood-framed television's flickering glow. Pop shows me my first slasher, John Carpenter's *Halloween*. He rests on the couch, chugging Coors cans and hocking loogies into a handkerchief as I sprawl on the shag carpet. Michael Myers chases Laurie Strode through a dark house. Laurie Strode stabs him in the neck with a knitting needle. Michael Myers keeps coming back from the dead. One day, Pop is taking a bath and his heart quits. Unlike Michael Myers, Pop stays dead.

Kristeva says the effect of observing a cadaver is akin to meeting a cripple.

The first time I see a real-life dead body is at my grandfather's funeral. During the service, I sit between Mom and my sister. Dad sits on the other side of the parlor with his new family. His girlfriend weeps like a cartoon. I do not speak to my father. A hearse drives Pop to the cemetery, and he goes into the ground. A few years later, the funeral home is sold and becomes a beauty salon.

The cripple disrupts order, glitches the system, confronts us with the limits of life. Disability triggers within the able-bodied an anxiety, a defense mechanism. At its most benign, this instinct manifests as apathy or smugness. The extreme reaction, of course, is a desire to exterminate. I cannot frighten you if I do not exist.

Before implementing the Final Solution, Nazi officials tested their gas chambers on the disabled population during a euthanasia campaign disguised under the innocuous name Charitable Foundation for Cure and Institutional Care—code name Aktion T4. Their logic was simple. "Defectives" could not work and were thus a strain on the Reich's precious resources. An estimated three hundred thousand people with disabilities were secretly executed before the end of World War II. *The work of salvation,* German doctors described their mission as.

Everyone I know is doing the Macarena. The sequence of dance moves first requires one to stick out their arms and then flip over their hands. I have to skip this part, which my friends at school delight in pointing out.

Make a choice. Is the cripple an object of pity or a source of inspiration? Shall you exploit or glorify the invalid? Are you entertained? Disgusted? Amused?

Lon Chaney paints his eye sockets black. He fixes jagged false teeth in his mouth. He pulls back his nose with wire.

When audiences first see him as the deformed Phantom of the Opera, they scream and faint in the movie theaters.

People are afraid of those who do not conform to their aesthetics.

Toward the end of the nineteenth century, legislation was passed in several American cities banning people with disabilities from being in public. In San Francisco, it was declared illegal for *any person who is diseased, maimed, mutilated or deformed in any way, so as to be an unsightly or disgusting object, to expose himself or herself to the public.* Those unlucky cripples who violated what were commonly known as the "ugly laws" could be fined, incarcerated, or sent to labor camps, all for spoiling the scenery.

The last documented arrest made for an ugly law violation occurred in 1974.

I go to Dusty's house. His parents are split, like mine, but he lives with his dad in a big new development instead of with his mom in a crumbling brick house downtown. Dusty's dad drives a Cadillac. Their fridge is stocked with thick cut bacon, marbled Black Angus steaks, butterscotch pudding cups—the kind of food my mother cannot afford. They have HBO. We play *Grand Theft Auto* and listen to

50 Cent on CD. Dusty says being able to rotate our hands is what separates us from the apes. He calls me Knuckle Walker, a superior grin on his chubby face, and gasps with laughter between gulps of pepperoni.

Twenty years later, I still walk with my hands in my pockets, afraid I look like an ape. Hands in pockets. Hands in lap. Hands behind back. Hands tucked under armpits.

Tsutomu enjoys watching the bloodiest films he can find, including the notorious *Guinea Pig* series, which depicts graphic scenes of torture. The plot of *Guinea Pig 2: Flower of Flesh and Blood* is straightforward. A man dressed as a samurai kidnaps and dismembers a nurse, cutting off her hands, feet, head. The special effects are realistic enough to convince Charlie Sheen he has watched a snuff film. He contacts the MPAA, who contact the FBI, and an investigation is launched. The director, Hideshi Hino, eventually demonstrates the gory makeup techniques as proof the on-screen murder is not real.

Stigma. Shame. Pressure to overcome obstacles. All reasons for many disabled people not to associate their impairment with disability, to distance themselves from the truth.

Before I began writing this book, I never once referred to myself as disabled. As if not acknowledging the truth might alter my reality.

To sway the general public in favor of euthanasia, the Nazi Party began a sustained campaign of propaganda. Numerous films were produced depicting the high cost of operating asylums for the incurably ill (sixty thousand reichsmark for a single cripple).

Ironically, Minister of Propaganda Joseph Goebbels was himself disabled. He had a deformed right foot, which forced him to wear a metal brace.

On weekends, Mom takes us to Wonder Book & Video. I pick up used copies of *Goosebumps* and scour through the stacks of horror VHS tapes, poring over the lurid cover art—bleeding skulls, rotting corpses, killer dolls—all lovingly painted by artists unknown. If the movie is in black-and-white, my mother considers it appropriate. I rent *Whatever Happened to Baby Jane?* I watch Bette Davis torture a paralyzed Joan Crawford, blanket pulled up to my chin, ready to shield my eyes if the movie gets too scary. I cannot look away.

Las Meninas has been widely analyzed but remains cryptic in some respects. Velázquez is ostensibly painting a portrait of the king and queen, who are reflected in a small mirror hanging on the wall. The figures stare back at us, as if the viewer and canvas have somehow swapped places. The composition implies that reality is only an illusion.

As is art.

As is disability.

Mom takes me and my sister to New York City when I'm eleven. Mom's youngest brother, my uncle, is getting married. My uncle is an actor, and the bride-to-be a dancer. The ceremony is held in a Midtown cathedral. The ushers kick out a cadre of bums sleeping in the pews. After the vows are said and done, we parade up Fifth Avenue to Central Park for the reception. A pristine September evening. We stay up past midnight eating and dancing and toasting the happy couple. There are cigars and dirty jokes and embarrassing family stories and wedding cake and Broadway gossip.

The next morning, back at our hotel, Mom wakes me up. I don't want to get out of bed. She whispers, *A plane flew into the World Trade Center.* I sit in front of the TV with

Mom and my sister and my grandmother. Nobody speaks. The footage is broadcast live. We see the second plane hit the South Tower. Little specks hesitate at the windows, then plummet to the ground—jumpers. We watch the tallest buildings on earth collapse. When we finally escape the city a few days later, I can still see the twin plumes of smoke hanging in the air.

An estimated 99 percent of occupants below the zone of impact in both World Trade Center towers survived the September 11 attacks. Of the remaining 1 percent on those lower floors who weren't so lucky, a high proportion were wheelchair users.

A blind man named Michael Hingson escaped the North Tower with the aid of his guide dog Roselle. Familiar with the building's emergency evacuation procedures, Hingson led his coworkers to safety down seventy-eight flights of stairs. That's 1,460 steps.

Sometimes, cripples can be useful.

The 1927 Supreme Court case *Buck v. Bell* legitimized the use of forced sterilization for those with intellectual disabilities. In the following decades, more than sixty-two thousand mental patients, mostly women, were made barren. The ruling supported a legal statute designed by the eugenicist Harry H. Laughlin, superintendent of the New York research institute Eugenics Record Office. The Nazis based their own Law for the Prevention of Hereditarily Diseased Offspring on this original statute, the Model Eugenical Sterilization Law, and admired Laughlin enough to award him an honorary doctorate from Heidelberg University in 1936. During the Nuremberg trials, Nazi doctors cited *Buck v. Bell* as a key part of their defense.

Sontag looks at Arbus's photographs of freaks and wonders how the subjects perceive themselves. Do they know how grotesque they are? Or are they oblivious to their ugliness?

Yes, Susan, the monster knows how ugly he is, because the rest of you never hesitate to tell him so.

And what of my hypothetical child? If the baby comes out wrong, how will I explain it to him, whatever his condition may be?

I am thirteen when American troops invade Iraq for the second time. Amid the saber-rattling, Mom takes me to see a specialist, at my request. She pulls me out of school early. We drive to Baltimore, the grimy urban sprawl a stark contrast to our own pastoral suburb. I study the massive Domino Sugar sign perched above the Inner Harbor. At the Johns Hopkins medical lab, I have X-rays taken of my arms. I see inside myself. The gray-haired doctor is all smiles and bad news. He pinches my elbow: *Your bones are fused together right here.* He points to the crook of my arm: *There is a cluster of nerves concentrated in the same spot. If we were to perform surgery, you would be left with permanent nerve damage. You would spend the rest of your life in constant pain. We would be able to give you only an extra inch of range; you would still be unable to fully rotate your hands.* Mom nods solemnly, rubs my back. I accept my fate.

The first victim of Aktion T4 was Gerhard Kretschmar, a child from Leipzig who was born blind, with one arm. His own parents petitioned to have him euthanized. Richard and Lina Kretschmar wrote directly to Adolf Hitler and requested permission to kill "the monster." The Führer complied, and Gerhard was soon euthanized. He was five months old.

Today, disabled children are twice as likely to experience physical or sexual violence and neglect.

Victims of trauma often perpetuate trauma. Does that excuse the monster's wrath?

Freaks effectively ended Browning's career. The film recorded a loss of more than $160,000, about $3 million in today's currency, and was pulled by MGM before completing its domestic run. It remained banned in the United Kingdom for thirty years.

I leave behind the baby fat of puberty. My body stretches. My hair grows long. I am good at making people laugh. My hands become a party trick. *Look at what I cannot do. Amazing, isn't it?* Matthew the Bilateral Boy—my own sideshow act performed in the basements of friends, the school cafeteria, the back seat of hand-me-down cars. Girls play with my hands, and I do not mind.

Cicero says, *In deformity and bodily disfigurement, there is good material for making jokes.*

Undeterred by his paralysis, Hob Broun commissioned a customized Franklin Ace 2000 computer attached to a sip-and-puff device. He wrote two books by blowing into a tube, activating the keyboard with each breath, producing letters on the screen. He literally breathed life into his work.

Entering high school, I take a plain white T-shirt, use iron-on letters to spell out the defect living within me: bilateral radioulnar synostosis. My tendency is to make fun of whatever discomforts me. I wear this cheeky fashion statement walking through the newly renovated hallways from classroom to classroom. Curious strangers stop to ask what it means, and when I explain, they remain confused.

When you see a disabled person, do you feel the urge to ask how it happened?

Freak shows trace their roots back to sixteenth-century England. Two of the most famed entertainers of that era were the Italian conjoined twins Lazarus and Joannes Baptista Colloredo, who performed for the court of King Charles I. Lazarus appeared courteous and handsome while Joannes's underdeveloped body dangled limply from his brother's chest. A parasitic twin, Joannes did not speak but would move if prodded. When Joannes was not on exhibition, Lazarus kept his brother concealed beneath a cloak to avoid unnecessary (and unpaid) attention. After touring Europe, Lazarus married and had several children, none of whom bore his mutation. He was later sentenced to death for murdering a man, but he staved off his execution by arguing that his innocent brother would also be killed.

Frank Henenlotter's 1982 cinematic sleaze masterpiece *Basket Case* tells the story of two brothers, Duane and

Belial. Conjoined at birth, they are involuntarily separated through surgery. Duane looks normal, but Belial is a hideously deformed lump of flesh, a head with two arms. Duane carries his brother in a large wicker basket through the seedy streets of Manhattan. They seek revenge on the doctor who ripped them apart, leaving a trail of mutilated corpses around Times Square.

I am sixteen when I get a job at Wonder Book & Video. The work is simple. Slap price stickers on stacks of books, put them on the shelves where they belong, show people where the titles they are looking for might be, ring up customers. I bring home a library's worth of volumes and decorate my room with yellowed paperbacks. My manager Kris buys me cigarettes and beer when I ask. He recommends movies for me to rent: *Check out Pasolini's* Salò. *It's fucked.* I start testing my limits.

Tsutomu becomes an *otaku*, what Americans might call a nerd, an obsessive collector, a fanboy caricature. Ignored, isolated, Tsutomu contemplates suicide. His grandfather acts as the socially maladjusted boy's only confidant. When the old man dies, Tsutomu is devastated. He secretly eats some of the crematory ashes as a way, Tsutomu later says, *to retain something from him.*

I can still smell Pop's cigarette smoke, taste the cold, sharp beer he let me try while we watched monster movies. He drank so much his legs went bad. Toward the end, he could barely walk. The biggest difference between us was not age but agency. Pop made himself a cripple. I never had a choice.

After being pulled from theaters, *Freaks* was censored and retitled *Nature's Mistakes*.

I thought God never made mistakes.

Sontag watches as the Grand Guignol cast of freaks is evicted from their underworld. No longer profitable, they become a nuisance. Displaced, the freak show seeks shelter, worming its way into the art scene. Here these living monstrosities find an air of legitimacy. But in art, the freak can be only a metaphor, eternally distant, inscrutable.

The monster is a metaphor for your deepest anxieties, your darkest desires. He wants love but is rejected for his ugliness. He rampages, murders those who have scorned him. You fear the monster, but you also pity him. He would not be evil unless he was heartbroken too.

Compassion. One of several factors the Nazis used to justify their euthanasia program.

My hands are starting to ache as I type. My wife suggests taking a break. She is right. If I overextend myself, I will only speed up the degeneration. When the day I can no longer write comes, I think I would prefer to be euthanized. To finally have a choice. Slashing my wrists would be inconvenient but not impossible.

On the other hand. Lend me a hand. Give me a hand. Need a hand. Got to hand it to you. A heavy hand. Empty hands. Red-handed. Hand off. Hand job. Hand jive. Try your hand. Tip your hand. Force your hand. Out of hand. Change of hand. Sleight of hand. Hand of cards. Hands of a clock. Hands of fate. Hands are tied. Hands down. Hand-me-down. Firsthand. Secondhand. Underhand. Overhand. Handyman. In good hands. Wash my hands of it. Take matters into my own hands. Know it like the back of my hand—but I only know the front of my hand.

Abjection as alien. Abjection as monster. Abjection as tumor. Abjection as cancer. Abjection as collapsed body. Abjection as failed language. Abjection as unconsciousness, deaf, dumb, mute.

I start dating in high school. One of my girlfriends is missing a hand. She came out wrong, like me. We bond over our shared limitations, swap tips on concealing our imperfections. She is red-haired, pale-skinned, beautiful if anatomically incomplete. We take MDMA and consecrate the trampoline in her backyard. The things she could do with that stump.

Several women I later dated have told me their friends often asked them what it was like to sleep with a cripple.

You tell me.

I spend a couple weeks hooking up with Heather. She's blonde and tan, with a hippie's disposition. We drink Bacardi and have sex on the rickety bed in her dad's guest room. I know her younger brother from theater classes. He was born with three toes on his left foot, an anomaly he delights in showing people. It's how he introduces himself: *Hi, I'm Sam, and I have three toes.* I break off the relationship with Heather before it gets serious. *I expected this*, she tells me. Years later, I learn Sam had corrective surgery. Some people can be fixed. Others aren't so lucky.

Tsutomu's sister catches him spying on her in the shower. When she confronts him, Tsutomu attacks her. Their mother learns of the altercation. She demands her son spend less time watching movies. She urges him to find a job. Tsutomu pummels his mother as well. He expands his collection to include hentai, hardcore splatter flicks, child pornography.

The monster wants to fuck. Nobody wants to fuck him. He is hideous, repulsive, abject. The monster sees the way you look at him. Treat him like a beast, and he will behave like one. Or was he simply born that way?

When I get my license, Nona gives me her old car. The Dodge Neon is a four-door gold sedan with a disconcertingly low safety rating. I keep Sharpies in the glove box and ask each new passenger to sign the Neon's ceiling. Soon it's covered with names, doodles, poems, caricatures, profanity, cartoons, proclamations, threats, cigarette burns, hearts, dicks. I drive the Neon everywhere. My girlfriend's beach house. Wonder Book & Video for work. Concerts in DC. Drug deals. Parties. One night I drink a handle of vodka and sit in the driver's seat parked behind Mom's house, and I call my ex and tell her I need to see her but I've lost the keys to my car, and when my ex shows up, she finds me lying in the driveway eating gravel and manages to drag me inside and tells Mom I'm drunk and puts me in bed, and I tell my ex how bad I want her back, and she calms me down and promises we can talk later, and when I wake up, I'm alone and sick, and I run to the bathroom and puke in the toilet, and as the fragments of the night surface, I know I owe my current girlfriend a call, and I tell her everything because I understand from experience it's better not to wait, and she calls me names I deserve to be called, and we break up over the phone, and I find my keys under the bed behind a stack of books, and I get in the Neon and drive into the mountains and get good and lost.

I stay lost for years.

Freaks is problematic. For all its portrayals of happy, functional, independent cripples, the titular freaks still become monsters at the end. In torrential rain they wade through thick mud, knives glinting. They pursue Cleopatra and Hercules, whose punishment is not death but worse. They carve up the lovers, disfigure them, making everyone equal. They tar and feather Cleopatra, gouge out an eye, snip her tongue, cut off her legs, mutilate her hands to look like webbed feet. The blonde bombshell is violently transformed into a human chicken. She squawks at the crowd. The carnival barker explains: *How she got that way will never be known. Some say it was a jealous lover. Others that it was the code of the freaks.*

While senators debated the particulars of the Americans with Disabilities Act, a group of crippled activists protested outside the Capitol. They abandoned crutches and wheelchairs, proceeding to drag their bodies up the one hundred stone steps. The stunt became known as the Capitol Crawl. One of these defiant cripples was Jennifer Keelan, a second grader with cerebral palsy who told reporters, *I'll take all night if I have to.*

Relentless. Like the knife-wielding dwarfs and amputees and pinheads. Crawling through the mud. Crawling up the Capitol. Monsters. Coming to get you.

Nazi doctors preserved hundreds of disabled children's brains in jars of formaldehyde and stored them for scientific study. A mad scientist's lab, like a scary movie—but real.

I start seeing a therapist during a bout of heavy depression when I'm seventeen. Dr. Ishtar prescribes me a generic version of Prozac. I quit taking it when I realize the side effects prevent me from coming. The meetings with Dr. Ishtar are unproductive. Half the time, I show up stoned on cold medicine. We talk about my parents' divorce being the crux of my abandonment issues. He doesn't tell me anything I don't already know. Dr. Ishtar insists on bringing my father in for a group session. Dad is all smiles, sitting cross-legged in the big leather chair. I tell him how he's hurt me and Mom and my sister. I tell him he makes me uncomfortable: *I'm your son, and you don't even know me.* He acts bemused. He doesn't understand what he's done wrong. He never apologizes. I stop visiting Dr. Ishtar.

August 22, 1988. Tsutomu's first victim is four-year-old Mari Konno. He lures her into his car and abducts her, takes her to a wooded area. He strangles and then rapes the girl. Tsutomu keeps her clothes and dismembers her hands and feet before disposing of the body. He chars some of the leftover pieces, grounds the bone into powder, and mails the remains to Mari's family. The package also contains several of the girl's teeth, photographs of her clothing, and a poem: *Mari. Cremated. Bones. Investigate. Prove.*

I lose sight of myself the year before I leave home for college in Boston. I break up with my one-handed girlfriend. I ditch school to get high in the woods. I am self-satisfying, hateful, apathetic. I hurt people and do not care. Somehow, I get cast in a local production of Martin McDonagh's *The Cripple of Inishmaan.* I am Billy Claven, a disabled orphan. My right arm is withered, and I walk with a limp. I live on the remote Aran Islands and dream of being a Hollywood star. One night, I do the show coming down from an acid trip. My acting is unhinged but convincing. I sob beneath the hot stage lights. I cough blood into a handkerchief. Am I faking it, though, if my performance is honest? I cannot tell the difference. I am a cripple playing a cripple, a monster pretending to be something else.

III

FIEND WITHOUT A FACE

Invisible disabilities are those that are not immediately apparent. An estimated 10 percent of Americans fall into this category, myself included.

Monsters can hide in plain sight. They live among us. Take our shape.

In John Carpenter's *The Thing*, an alien creature adopts the form of whatever it consumes—first dogs, then humans. A perfect mimic. When threatened, the Thing abandons this facade, morphing into all manner of tentacled abominations. A man with oozing claws for hands. A severed head running around on spindly spider legs. A stomach split into gaping jaws. How easily the body is replicated, corrupted.

If the monster might be anybody, who can we trust?

Mom drives me eight hours across four states up to Boston. I am here to study film at Emerson College. NYU was my first choice, but they turned me down. Mom helps me unload the big plastic bins full of clothes, books, toiletries. She doesn't know I brought half an ounce of pot hidden in some socks. I'm living right across from the Boston Common, with its statues of revolutionary heroes and towering elms. We have dinner at an Italian restaurant. Over a steaming plate of fettuccine Mom says, *You can always call if you need anything.* I promise I will, eyeballing an open bottle of red wine at an adjacent table. Mom rarely gets emotional. She is stoicism personified. I know she will miss me. She doesn't cry. She says, *I just want you to be happy.* Mom is spending thousands of dollars she doesn't have so I can learn about making movies. I'm too snot-nosed to appreciate it. *I am happy*, I lie.

Lord Byron's mother, the wealthy Scottish heiress Catherine Gordon, described her son as a *lame brat*. Byron was born with a deformed right foot that caused him to limp throughout his life. He was supposedly self-conscious of his clubfoot and wore special shoes with wide trousers to conceal the defect. He refused to wear a leg brace, nicknaming himself Le Diable Boîteux—the limping devil. Those who knew him remarked the limp was barely noticeable.

When people look at me, is it obvious?

Frida Kahlo's life was marked by illness and injury. Some historians speculate she was born with spina bifida, a condition in which the spine fails to develop properly. What is certain is that Frida contracted polio when she was six years old. Her right leg shriveled and became noticeably thinner than the left. Poor circulation in her bad leg caused chronic pain for the duration of Frida's life. She hid her deformity beneath fabric, telling a friend, *I must have full skirts and long, now that my sick leg is so ugly.*

I prefer long-sleeved shirts myself.

Nazi officials took great care to cloak their euthanasia program. Cripples were not ordered to be killed—they were assigned "special treatment," what the Nazis called *Sonderbehandlung*. The condemned were transported from their residences in "charitable ambulances" operated by SS men disguised in white coats to appear less threatening. Patients were promised better living conditions at T4 clinics. Most would be dead within twenty-four hours of their arrival, lured into gas chambers made to look like showers. Their bodies were cremated, a random sample of ashes sent to the families. Wartime conditions provided the perfect excuse to bar inquisitive relatives from snooping. Doctors operating the facilities spent the majority of their time creating thousands of falsified death certificates.

Attitudes persist in the United States today that Social Security fraud is rampant, costing taxpayers untold billions of dollars. The Social Security Administration, though, flags fewer than 1 percent of disability claims as fraudulent. A mere 4 percent of the American working-age population claim disability benefits. Meanwhile, the average American has a one in three chance of dying or becoming disabled before retirement.

In 2015, a Philadelphia woman named Linda Weston pled guilty to 196 criminal counts, including charges of murder, kidnapping, sex trafficking, hate crimes, forced labor, and benefits fraud. For a decade straight, Weston and several accomplices preyed upon those with mental disabilities across four states. They coaxed vulnerable individuals with promises of shelter and care, then confined and manipulated victims to collect their Social Security benefits, extorting more than $200,000 before they were finally caught. They locked their captives in basements, attics, or closets, frequently beating them with sticks, bats, hammers, guns. The prisoners were fed a steady diet of beans or ramen noodles laced with sedatives. When food was scarce, they were forced to eat human waste. At least two of Weston's victims died from malnourishment.

I'm good at finding allies. I meet some girls on my dorm floor. I show them my pot sock. We go hook up with some other kids they know in the Common. I'm the only one holding and that makes me everyone's new best friend. We sit in a circle under a tree, passing my bowl in the dark. Milo, a sheepish stoner, introduces me to his friend Jill. She wears a long teal scarf, a silver hoop in her nose. She lets me hold her hand.

October 3, 1988. Tsutomu is driving along a rural road when he picks up seven-year-old Masami Yoshizawa. He parks at the same spot where he murdered Mari Konno and does the same things to Masami.

Peter Medak's 1980 film *The Changeling* follows a composer named John Russell, played by George C. Scott, who moves into a Victorian-style mansion after the death of his wife and daughter in a car accident. Russell begins hearing strange noises and suspects the house is haunted. A red ball continually materializes, even after Russell throws it off a bridge. The spirit trying to contact him is revealed to be that of a crippled boy who had been kept hidden in the attic. Fearing the child won't survive into adulthood—thus forfeiting the inheritance willed to him by his grandfather—the boy's own father drowned him in a bathtub, later replacing him with an orphaned child, a better model, a changeling. With Russell's help, the ghost has his revenge, killing his double and burning the cursed house down. In the final frame, we see the boy's wheelchair sitting among the charred ruins. He has been freed.

Some disabilities are permanent. Others are temporary.

The German watchmaker Stephan Farffler, a paraplegic, created the first self-propelled wheelchair in 1655. The three-wheeled carriage was operated with a simple hand crank. Nearly one hundred years later, the British inventor James Heath improved upon the design, naming his model the Bath chair, after his hometown. By the nineteenth century, this proto-wheelchair was commonly referred to as the "invalid carriage."

Invalid from the Latin *invalidus*, "infirm," "impotent," "weak," "feeble."

Dr. Hermann Pfannmüller, an early advocate of the Nazi euthanasia program, says, *It is unbearable to me that the flower of our youth must lose their lives at the front, while that feeble-minded and asocial element can have a secure existence in the asylum.*

How do you measure a person's worth? Strength? Ability? Fortitude? I wish I wasn't so weak. Physically. Because of my condition, I've never been much of a weight lifter. I've never been much of an anything lifter.

Composed between 1812 and 1819, Francisco Goya's painting *The Madhouse* offers a bleak view of humanity. Inside a cavernous chamber, a congregation of lunatics has been imprisoned. They crowd together beneath a barred window, the only light source. Mostly naked, some wear clever symbols—a feather headdress, a tricorn hat, a crown. One man holds bull horns against his scalp. Another appears ready to plunge a dagger into his cellmate's neck. Many of the figures are obscured by shadow. Featureless. Indistinct. A mass of bodies without reason.

I wonder, might I have been kept in a place like that?

Goya claimed to have based the painting on a scene he witnessed at a Zaragoza mental asylum. For centuries it was not uncommon to find disabled persons lumped alongside criminals, shackled with iron chains, subjected to rampant abuse. Goya himself had suffered a serious bout of depression and mania not long before starting work on *The Madhouse*, conditions that would plague the artist for the remainder of his life.

I rent a camera for my first student film project. The plot revolves around a man who is making a snuff movie. I cast my friend Sid as the lead. He's one of the few people I've met in Boston who's even wilder than me. I play the victim. Jill helps out behind the scenes. She binds my hands, ties a bag over my head. I pretend to suffocate on camera. We review the footage. Jill says it doesn't look real enough. I tell her to tie the bag tighter, make it so I can't breathe. I almost lose consciousness, but we get the shot. When I screen the final cut, my professor is unimpressed. After class, Sid and I go to the Common and get high under a bridge near the swan boats. We agree to make our next attempt even more revolting.

From 1969 to 1971, Diane Arbus regularly crossed the Hudson to photograph asylum residents in neighboring New Jersey. Her most frequented destination was an all-female institution located in the city of Vineland. She exposed almost two thousand frames of film from those trips, haunting images of mentally disabled women posing in barren fields under gray skies. Arbus would visit on holidays to capture mental patients donned in Easter bonnets and handmade Halloween costumes. The untitled scenes have a dreamlike quality, accentuated by soft, flat lighting and a disconcerting combination of blurred and sharp focus. Her subjects smile, wearing crudely fashioned masks, marching in procession to who knows where. In stark contrast to other contemporary photojournalism that documents people with disabilities, Arbus depicts her subjects in a state of happiness and joy rather than anguish and despair.

In a letter to a friend, Arbus wrote of her desire to photograph people she described as retards, imbeciles, idiots, and morons, especially cheerful ones.

The monster is easier to swallow when he smiles.

My RAs bust me for smoking in my dorm. Rebecca, a senior, is a squat musical-theater major whom I loathe. Casey is a junior studying sports journalism. He dreams of becoming the Red Sox announcer. I find him slightly more sympathetic than Rebecca. After they write me up, I get put on academic probation. I'm required to see a counselor once a week. Any other transgressions and I'll be expelled. In retaliation, I declare war on the fifth floor. Rebecca spends hours meticulously creating displays on a long corkboard in the hallways. Event fliers, holiday decorations, drivel. In the early morning hours while most everyone is still asleep, I take to slashing apart Rebecca's handiwork with a folding knife I always carry. I shred the cardstock leaves of her autumn-social spread, embed deep gashes in the poster for the student production of *Rent* she's directing. I also make a habit of vandalizing the bathrooms, tearing doors off stalls, scratching the mirrors, graffitiing obscenities on the walls. *I'll be back but you won't know when, the Shithouse Poet strikes again!*

Would Byron's poetry be so well remembered had his clubfoot not caused him constant misery? Did suffering infuse his verse with the stuff of immortality?

In his 1612 essay "Of Deformity," the English philosopher Francis Bacon argues that people with deformities are even with nature, *for as nature hath done ill by them, so do they by nature; being for the most part (as the Scripture saith) void of natural affection; and so they have their revenge of nature.*

I wouldn't say I'm resentful about being a cripple. Most of the time.

I wouldn't say I'm void of affection. Most of the time.

Shakespeare's version of Richard III is a disfigured hunchback. He feels cheated by fate, turns bitter, tells the audience in his opening soliloquy, *I am determined to prove a villain / And hate the idle pleasures of these days.* The trope of the deformed antagonist has always existed, but

Shakespeare's King Richard is a unique case. He is articulate, clever, darkly humorous. Despite his wickedness, we sympathize with Richard, who forges that connection by speaking directly to us. He is cripple as antihero. Still, he must die at the end.

The American lawyer Clarence Darrow, most famous for being the defense attorney during the Scopes Monkey Trial of 1925, once suggested: *Chloroform unfit children. Show them the same mercy that is shown beasts that are no longer fit to live.*

What the Nazis called *Lebensunwertes Leben,* "life unworthy of life."

Of Boston I remember huddling in circles outside the dorm building's entrance, passing around cigarettes. I remember a girl who used to keep a hedgehog inside her sweater pocket. I remember getting busted for drinking at a Chinese karaoke joint. I remember taking classes with Denis Leary's son and finding him unremarkable. I remember a short-haired butch lesbian who sold me the best weed at the best price. I remember almost getting arrested by mounted Boston Police Department officers for trying to smoke said weed in a cemetery for Revolutionary War heroes. I remember catching athlete's foot when I forgot to wear flip-flops in the communal shower. I remember watching *Lost* with Jill on her laptop. I remember my friend Milo coming out to me, how relieved he was when I wasn't weird about it. I remember M.I.A.'s "Paper Planes" playing at every party. I remember a kid who told me he was born with a congenital heart defect and didn't know how much longer he had to live. I remember little of what went on in the classes I occasionally bothered to attend.

David Cronenberg's 1979 film *The Brood* tells the story of a divorced couple, Frank and Nola Carveth, who are embroiled in a custody battle over their daughter Candice. Having undergone an experimental form of psychother-apy, Nola begins to asexually produce deformed, dwarflike creatures in an external womb, the physical manifestation of her darkest emotions—anxiety, fear, hatred. Psychically linked to Nola, the creatures begin butchering anyone who becomes the subject of their mother's rage. When a desperate Frank strangles Nola to death, so too does her brood expire.

A 530,000-year-old deformed skull discovered in a Span-ish cave suggests that early hominids were capable of caring for disabled kin. Located in an archaeological site known as Sima de los Huesos— the Pit of Bones—the skull belonged to a ten-year-old boy of the species *Homo heidelbergensis.* He suffered from the birth defect cranio-synostosis, which causes joints in the skull to fuse before the brain can finish growing, severely impairing intellectual development. The boy would have needed special care to survive as long as he did.

Empathy, then, is as ancient as cruelty.

The circus is in town. I call Mom and ask to borrow some money so I can buy a pair of tickets. I tell her it's going to be a surprise for my girlfriend. My romanticism amuses Mom, and she wires exactly enough cash into my account. Later, I'm walking through the Common with Jill. I point out the garish red-and-white big top at the park's edge. I ask Jill if she's afraid of clowns, and she laughs: *I'm from Jersey. I'm not afraid of anything.* I pull out the tickets, and she keeps laughing: *What kind of guy takes his girlfriend to the circus?* Soon we're snuggled up on the bleachers, picking popcorn shards from our gums. The ringleader, with his top hat and tails, starts the show. Ponies decked in ornate saddles rip around the space, nimble gymnasts leaping from one beast to the next. Clowns in their baggy tramp outfits and painted faces descend upon the audience, razzing a meathead Boston cop whose children start wailing. Trapeze artists swing overhead, bedazzled leotards twinkling chaotic under hot stage lights. An elephant rears on its hind legs, its outstretched trunk trumpeting thunder. The human cannonball is blasted up, up, and away. There are no freaks, but the spectacle is plenty horrific.

The actress Olga Baclanova, who played Cleopatra in *Freaks*, was initially disturbed upon meeting her cast-mates: *I wanted to cry when I saw them. They have such nice faces, but it is so terrible . . . Now, after we start the picture, I like them all so much.*

Sexual attraction to disabilities is called devotism. Within this niche fetish community, amputations and prostheses are the most popular turn-ons.

The ancient Egyptians are credited with designing the first artificial limbs. Archaeologists found a sophisticated wooden toe dating back to the fifteenth century B.C.E. The Egyptians believed that amputations would carry on into the afterlife. Missing body parts had to be replaced and buried with the dead.

When she was only twenty-one, the American perfor-mance artist Lisa Bufano had her lower legs and most of her fingers amputated after catching a staph infec-tion. Undeterred, she pursued a career in dance. Using a customized set of Queen Anne table legs as prosthetics,

Bufano toured the world in a number of original productions. Her signature piece, *Five Open Mouths*, was named after the stubs on her hands.

Dozens of prehistoric cave dwellings scattered throughout France and Spain contain stencils of human hands. Some of these negative imprints have missing fingers.

Part of my academic probation requires that I enroll in therapy sessions. I sit down with the school psychiatrist once a week. She asks about my family life, my history of substance abuse, my emotional state. I tell her what I expect she wants to hear: *I don't do this often. It's not a habit. No, I wouldn't say that I self-medicate. I'm not depressed.* I'm a convincing actor. She takes notes. I leave the office and meet Milo and Jill. We get high in the Common and walk up Newbury. We drink coffee and smoke cigarettes and talk shit—the finest therapy money can buy.

Thousands of disabled patients began disappearing from German hospitals. People noticed. They watched busloads of inmates transported from asylums. They saw smoke billow from crematorium chimneys. They observed the same buses returning empty. In the town of Hadamar, ashes clumped with human hair rained down on the increasingly suspicious populace. Hospital staff, drinking themselves into oblivion at local taverns, let secrets slip. Soon, it became common knowledge. The new T4 "charitable institutes" were in fact killing centers. Children chased buses with blacked-out windows through the streets, shouting, *Here are some more coming to be gassed!*

For the most part, I move through the world without receiving judgment, pity, or revulsion in a way that is impossible for someone who uses a wheelchair. Only when people spend a prolonged period of time with me does the smokescreen begin to dissipate.

September 17, 1925. Mexico City. An overcast day. Light rain. Frida Kahlo and her boyfriend Alejandro Gómez Arias tire of wandering the streets downtown. They catch a bus heading toward Coyoacán—home. Frida realizes she forgot her umbrella. The couple hop off to retrieve it and board the next bus. A fateful decision. The second bus is new, its wood frame brightly painted, two long benches on each side. Near full. Frida and Alex find seats in the back. Turning onto the Calzada de Tlalpan, the bus driver attempts to pass an oncoming electric streetcar. He doesn't make it. The trolley crashes into the side of the bus, dragging it along the tracks before splitting the frame in two. Alex is caught under the train but suffers only minor injuries. A few passengers lie dead among the wreckage.

Alex finds Frida nude, the clothes torn from her body in the accident. She's been covered in powdered gold from the ripped bag of a house painter who was riding the bus. Gold mixes with blood. Onlookers cry, *¡La bailarina!* They think Frida's a dancer.

Lisa Bufano says, *Despite my own terror and discomfort in being watched (or, maybe, because of it), I am finding that being in front of viewers as a performer with deformity can produce a magnetic tension that could be developed into strength.*

The monster watches you watching him. He knows you revile him. But he knows, too, how he fascinates you. This is the monster's power. He hypnotizes you so that he may have his way with you.

An iron handrail from the streetcar has found its way into Frida's pelvis. Alex and another man pull the bar from Frida's flesh. Her screams are louder than the approaching ambulance's siren. At the hospital, doctors doubt Frida will survive. The injuries are extensive. Fractured pelvic bone, punctured abdomen and uterus, spine broken in three places, right leg broken in eleven places, vertebrae displaced, right foot crushed and dislocated, broken collarbone, dislocated shoulder. She is in the hospital bed for a full month, but Frida does not die. *Like a sword through a bull,* she describes the pain as.

I hate to admit when my wrists hurt, a daily occurrence. When I turn a doorknob. When I lift a mug to my lips. When I hold a book.

Kristeva says abjection, especially abjection of the self, is predicated on desire. Recognition of this irrepressible want stirs the abjection within us. Language and meaning, our very being, is a consequence of yearning. In my case, a desire to face my palms to heaven.

The book of John recounts a miracle. Jesus and his disciples passed a blind beggar in the streets of Jerusalem. The disciples asked, *Who sinned, this man or his parents, that he was born blind?* Before healing the beggar, Jesus answered, *This man didn't sin, nor did his parents, but that the works of God might be revealed in him.*

How might God reveal his work in me?

In "Faith Poem," Walt Whitman wrote, *I do not doubt there is far more in trivialities, / insects, vulgar persons, slaves, dwarfs, weeds, / rejected refuse, than I have supposed.*

December 12, 1988. Tsutomu kidnaps four-year-old Erika Namba, who is walking home from a friend's house. Tsutomu drives to a parking lot, where he strips the girl and takes photographs before killing her. He binds her hands and feet behind her back and ditches the body in another parking lot. Tsutomu sends a poem to Erika's family: *Erika. Cold. Cough. Throat. Rest. Death.*

I get a job through some vague nonprofit attached to the college. This will be my first time teaching, although I don't realize it when I sign up for the gig. In a sterile and brutishly bureaucratic building on Boylston, I'm dropped in a room full of immigrants and instructed to teach them basic English. I have no professional training. I stand beside a wide whiteboard and write simple words and phrases with a dying dry-erase marker. Seated around the stuffy classroom are tiny old men from Honduras and El Salvador, quiet and attentive young beauties from Egypt and Palestine wearing crisp hijabs, pensive and pimply-skinned exchange students from Hong Kong and South Korea. *Hello,* I say. *Hello,* they answer. *Good. That's a start. How are you?* I ask. *Okay, fine, very well, thank you,* they reply. I hold up a sheet of ruled paper and say, *Paper.* I hold up a pencil and say, *Pencil. Pen-cil. Yes?* Everyone smiles and nods. After a week of this, I quit without notice.

In the 110-minute running time of Nicolas Roeg's *Don't Look Now*, the killer is on-screen for thirty seconds with zero dialogue. At the film's climax, John Baxter, played by Donald Sutherland, corners who he thinks is the phantom of his drowned daughter. But no, the short-statured figure in the bright red coat he's been chasing is not his little girl. She is a wizened, knife-wielding dwarf—the serial killer who's been prowling the canals of Venice. Her motives are ambiguous, as is her reaction to confronting Baxter in the church he's been restoring. She shakes her head as if to say, *No, I'm sorry, you've got it all wrong*, before slicing Baxter's throat. Grief transfigured into horror, the little girl into a hideous monster. Should've seen it coming.

I wonder whether my parents would've had second thoughts if they'd known how I'd come out.

The famed disability rights activist Helen Keller spent decades traveling the world on behalf of the American Foundation for the Blind as an advocate for those living with vision loss. She was also a staunch supporter of eugenics, writing in favor of euthanasia for infants born with severe mental impairments or physical deformities. She believed their lives to be worthless, that they would grow up to be criminals. In her own words, *Our puny sentimentalism has caused us to forget that a human life is sacred only when it may be of some use to itself and to the world.* Miracle worker, indeed.

Euthanasia literally means "a good death."

Before the widespread use of poisonous gas, most victims of the Nazi euthanasia program were given lethal injections, typically phenol. Some Nazi doctors preferred killing patients by gradually reducing their food, which they considered more humane.

Agustí Villaronga's 1986 film *In a Glass Cage* follows Klaus, a former Nazi doctor who performs sadomasochistic experiments on children in concentration camps. After the war he flees to a remote Catalonian village, where he continues abducting young boys to rape, torture, and kill. When his crimes are discovered, he leaps from a tower, but the suicide attempt fails. Klaus is left paralyzed, confined to an iron lung.

I visit the Boston Public Library every week to borrow movies. The selection is impressive: Russian art house, Spanish splatter punk, J-horror, atomic age sci-fi. The assignments my professors dole out are always an afterthought; this is my real homework. I load the DVDs into my laptop and copy the files onto a hard drive. I make my own pirated library. At night, I smoke in the Common, return to my room, and marathon the latest haul. My roommate Saif is never there. He has an apartment. His father is an obscenely wealthy manufacturing mogul from Dubai. Saif reserved a dorm mostly for kicks. *In case I need a place to study*, he explains. Saif would throw his clothes away after wearing them once. I pluck his discarded Armani and Chanel from the trash can. We do share one affinity—ditching class.

Painted toward the end of his life, *Self-Portrait with Dr. Arrieta* depicts Francisco Goya in the realm between life and death. An earlier, undiagnosed illness had left Goya deaf by 1793. A second unknown ailment came close to killing him in 1819. Historians speculate that Goya may have suffered from a range of diseases—syphilis, lead poisoning, encephalitis, stroke. Under Dr. Arrieta's care, Goya was nursed back to health, surviving another eight years. This final self-portrait was Goya's gift to the good doctor.

I remember a doctor asking what exactly my condition prevented me from doing. I had trouble answering. It is difficult to verbalize a lifetime's worth of incapacity.

The inscription written on the bottom of the canvas reads, *Goya gives thanks to his friend Arrieta for the expert care with which he saved his life from an acute and dangerous illness which he suffered at the close of the year 1819 when he was seventy-three years old. He painted it in 1820.* The scene portrays a weakened Goya feebly clutching at his bedsheets as Dr. Arrieta coaxes his patient to drink a glass of medicine. Behind the pair lurk three shadowy figures. Literal interpretations suggest that they are concerned bystanders, neighbors perhaps, or priests preparing the final sacrament. Others take a more metaphysical approach, viewing the onlookers as feverish manifestations, demons signaling the artist's destruction.

June 1, 1973. Twenty-eight-year-old British musician Robert Wyatt falls from a fourth-floor bathroom window during a party in London's posh Maida Vale neighborhood. He wakes in a hospital bed, where he spends the next three months recuperating. The fall leaves Wyatt paralyzed from the waist down. Wyatt recalls his relief at being too drunk to feel any pain, like a bullfighter getting loaded before entering the arena or a soldier emptying his flask before charging the enemy, *people who are smashed getting smashed.*

Alcoholism is linked to high blood pressure, heart disease, stroke, liver disease, and digestive problems, as well as cancer of the breast, mouth, throat, esophagus, liver, and colon, not to mention a bevy of depression and anxiety disorders. The Social Security Administration does not consider chronic alcohol use disorder a disability.

Tell that to my father. And his father. And his father. And my mother's father.

A few months before his trip out the window, Wyatt was in Venice with his girlfriend Alfreda "Alfie" Benge, who was working as an assistant editor on *Don't Look Now*. She bought Wyatt an inexpensive Riviera organ to occupy him. Inspired by the city's wide canals, Wyatt began composing music for what would become the album *Rock Bottom*.

It's okay . . . It's okay . . . I'm a friend . . . I won't hurt you . . . Come on . . . Wait . . . Wait.

IV

HOW TO MAKE A MONSTER

Toward the semester's end, I take a bus to Brooklyn. My
friend Jules is living in Jamaica Heights, studying film, like
me, but mostly fucking around and getting stoned, like me.
We rendezvous with Vic, completing the tight-knit trio
we formed during high school. We're ostensibly planning
to celebrate Vic's birthday. For the occasion Jules scores
acid from Cindy, an older acquaintance from back home
who's studying photography in Manhattan. We swallow
the tabs at Cindy's place before taking the metro back
across the water. When we make it to Jules's apartment,
the acid kicks in. The walls bleed. I'm covered in blood.
I'm screaming. Time distends and I find myself hurtled
decades into the past, then the future. I become undone.
I see twisted faces in surgical masks warping, decaying.
Heads split gristly gray brains and reform themselves
again in an infinite nightmare loop. Incomprehensible
voices boom and echo. I am lost. When I come out of the
black, I find myself in a hospital bed, an IV in my arm.
I've pissed myself. I stand, unsteady, and wander into the
hallway where a Dominican nurse chastises me, guides me

back to my room. Somehow Mom appears with sad, worried eyes. Unsure what is and isn't real, I'm bundled into a car and driven four hours back to Maryland, where I fall into my old bed and sleep for two days straight.

Marcel Proust spent the last three years of his life mostly bedridden, hardly leaving his room at 44 rue Hamelin in Paris, finishing the last volumes of *In Search of Lost Time*.

The four-thousand-year-old remains of a crippled man were discovered at the Neolithic archaeological site Mán Bạc, located in northern Vietnam. Dubbed "Burial 9," the skeleton showed signs of Klippel-Feil syndrome, a genetic disease that causes spinal bones to fuse, resulting in paralysis. As part of a small group of Stone Age hunter-gatherers, Burial 9 survived well into his mid-twenties. Despite his offering no contributions to the tribe, someone must have cared for this man. Someone must have cared.

The renowned religious reformer Martin Luther was once asked his opinion regarding the strange case of a disabled twelve-year-old boy from the city of Dessau, who was said to do nothing but ceaselessly eat and excrete. Luther suggested the boy be suffocated or drowned. When asked for what reason, Luther replied, *Because I think he's simply a mass of flesh without a soul. Couldn't the devil have done this,*

*inasmuch as he gives such shape to the body and mind even of
those who have reason that in their obsession they hear, see, and
feel nothing? The devil is himself their soul.*

Some religious leaders resisted the Nazi euthanasia program. The Lutheran theologian Friedrich von
Bodelschwingh, who served as director of the Bethel
Institution for Epilepsy at Bielefeld, repeatedly refused to
turn over his patients to the Gestapo. He was imprisoned
for three months. A sympathetic bishop, Clemens Graf
von Galen, defied the regime to deliver a public sermon
in protest against the euthanasia campaign: *And now the
fifth commandment: "Thou shalt not kill," is set aside and broken under the eyes of the authorities whose function it should
be to protect the rule of law and human life when men presume
to kill innocent fellow-men with intent merely because they are
"unproductive."*

The Seven Works of Mercy is a series of panel-mounted oil
paintings composed by the Master of Alkmaar in 1504.
Each piece depicts the corporal works of mercy—feeding
the hungry, giving drink to the thirsty, clothing the naked,
burying the dead, sheltering the traveler, comforting the
sick, ransoming the captive. The first panel features a man
with underdeveloped legs sitting on the ground. He sup-
ports himself with a handheld, three-legged crutch, his

free hand reaching for a loaf of bread, a sullen expression on his face. Along with women, disabled and deformed persons were considered the worthiest of charity.

Any memory of that night in Brooklyn eludes me. When I emerge from hibernation I meet with Jules, who has likewise left behind the big city and retreated home. We walk together beside a still creek gone scummy with algae and duck shit. I tell Jules my mind is blank. He fills me in. Not long after we returned to his apartment, Jules says I freaked out, started screaming, clawing the walls. I demanded he call an ambulance. The NYPD arrived first. I picked up the television and threw it at the cops, who promptly restrained me. I was strapped onto a gurney and put in the back of an ambulance. Before they closed the doors, I said, *Jules, I'm going to kill you.* You know the rest. Traumatized, Jules abandoned any prospects he had going and fled, dropping out of school and moving back in with his parents, the unforeseen consequences of my first and last bad trip.

August 23, 2020, 5:11 P.M. Police in Kenosha, Wisconsin, respond to a 911 call reporting family trouble. Less than five minutes later, officer Rusten Sheskey puts seven bullets in Jacob Blake's back. Blake survives but is left paralyzed from the waist down. Extensive organ damage.

Most of Blake's small intestine has to be removed. He is initially handcuffed to his hospital bed before posting bond. No officers are charged.

I wonder what would have happened to me if my skin were the same color as Jacob Blake's.

As in most facets of American society, racial disparities exist among disabled people. Nine percent of white workers report having disabilities, compared to 11 percent of Black workers.

Harriet Tubman suffered from epilepsy as the result of severe head trauma incurred when she was twelve years old during a beating from her master.

In 1835, P. T. Barnum began a new exhibition: Joice Heth, slave of Augustine Washington, whose son George led his country to victory and freedom. Yes, Joice Heth, the most astonishing curiosity in the world, raised our founding father from infancy. She clothed the boy, fed him, rocked him to sleep against her bosom. Joice Heth, born 1674 and still with us today. That's right, folks, the woman you see before you has arrived at the astonishing age of 161 years!

Enfreakment refers to a process of silencing, stylizing, and commercializing the extraordinary body through exhibition.

Joice Heth certainly looked the part. Small-framed with deep wrinkles, she was blind and mostly paralyzed, with fingernails like talons. Barnum had her teeth removed to bolster the effect. She could still speak. She would tell the crowd stories about little George. The truth is that Joice Heth was only about eighty years old when she was sold to P. T. Barnum. She died less than a year later. To assuage skeptics, Barnum held a public autopsy before a crowd of fifteen hundred in New York City, charging fifty cents admission. The surgeon declared fraud. Barnum claimed the body was not actually Heth's. She was alive and well, traveling through Europe. He later admitted to the hoax.

Susan Sontag does not believe America is a freak show. Too easy a metaphor. As Americans, though, we are partial to myths, seduced by stories of redemption and damnation alike. The freak endures, and our fascination with his fate will never be sated.

Jill visits over winter break. I spill the whole story. I can't tell if she feels sorry for me or is simply disgusted. She meets my family. My sister Marie doesn't like Jill, says she's boring. She has license to be wary. Most of my girl-friends have at some point or other used Marie to get to me, a means to an end. So far I've been reckless and often heartless in my relationships. I'm a cheater, like Dad. I discard one girl for the next with little regard for their feelings. The monster is a selfish creature, driven by lust. After a week Jill takes a bus back to New Jersey. One night I call my ex and invite her over.

In the fifth canto of *Inferno*, Dante and Virgil observe the second circle of hell. The sinners there are guilty of lust, trapped inside a never-ending whirlwind. Dante calls out to Francesca da Rimini, who was forced into an arranged marriage as a way to broker peace between two warring families. Francesca's husband, Giovanni Malatesta, is wealthy but deformed. He is called Giovanni the Lame or simply Lo Zoppo—the cripple. Francesca falls in love with Giovanni's younger brother Paolo. The affair lasts a decade, until Giovanni surprises the pair in Frances-ca's bedroom. Lo Zoppo's hands must have worked well enough. He kills his wife and brother with a rapier. Fran-cesca tells Dante, *Love led the two of us to one death.*

Why damn the lovers but not the murderous cripple? Is the deformity punishment enough?

Four years after the bus accident, Frida Kahlo marries Diego Rivera. Twenty years her senior, Rivera is already an established artist. Apprehensive at first, Frida's parents soon give the couple their blessing. Rivera is wealthy and Frida needs financial support. She is unable to work because of her injuries. Frequent trips to the doctor do not come cheap. They soon move to the rural state of Morelos, where Frida begins sporting her signature wardrobe— long, colorful skirts that show off her mestiza ancestry. Plus, they are perfect for hiding the scars.

Around the time she quit her day job as a fashion photographer to focus on her own work, Diane Arbus settled into a prolonged depression. Her marriage collapsed. She had a bout of hepatitis. She likened the experience to *a spiritual automobile accident.*

J. G. Ballard's 1973 novel *Crash* revolves around a group of extreme sexual fetishists led by the enigmatic Dr. Robert Vaughan, whose followers play out perverse games, reenacting famous celebrity car crashes or deliberately wrecking their automobiles to get off on the subsequent destruction. Narrator James Ballard, named after the author himself, enters a relationship with a woman named Gabrielle, whose body has been ravaged by severe vehicular trauma. Her deformities become analogous to the sexual excitement latent within acts of violence, Ballard tells us, recounting the orgasmic pleasure of penetrating a deep wound on Gabrielle's thigh.

Handicapable, no?

Infamous pornographer Larry Flynt joined the disabled community on March 6, 1978. During an obscenity trial in Lawrenceville, Georgia, a gunman attacked Flynt and his lawyer as they walked to the courthouse. The shooter was Joseph Paul Franklin, a white supremacist serial killer who traveled the country targeting Black and Jewish people, seeking to "cleanse the world." Franklin had been outraged by an interracial photospread in Flynt's flagship *Hustler* magazine. He used a Marlin .44 rifle, a high-caliber weapon typically reserved for big-game hunting. Flynt took a bullet to the spine and was left paralyzed, later bound to a gold-plated wheelchair. Franklin was never charged for the shooting but was executed for his other crimes in 2013. Flynt opposed the decision, stating, *I firmly believe that a government that forbids killing among its citizens should not be in the business of killing people itself.*

Disability rights activist Stella Young coined the phrase *inspiration porn*, the feel-good depiction of cripples who defy their disability. Her criticisms suggest that these seemingly positive portrayals dehumanize disabled people by reducing them to examples of exceptionalism, effectively othering disability as a burden to overcome.

It's been a few years since she found the messages from another girl on my phone, so Liane is speaking to me again. A buddy's older brother buys me a thirty-pack, and I'm sharing the cans with Liane and bragging about my bad acid trip. I stick *Evil Dead* into the VCR. Liane asks why I still use tapes, and I explain how analog is a superior format. *Plus, horror movies are collectibles,* I say. We don't pay much attention to the screen. We talk and talk and drink and drink, and soon we're reminiscing over old times and the way things used to be and wondering why we ever split. We end up in my bed, and I'm taking her clothes off and we're kissing, and she knows about Jill because I told her earlier, and Liane's saying, *No, we shouldn't do this.* I keep kissing her, slurring my words, *I want you.* She says, *Matt, stop,* and I do, rolling over beside her and passing out before she can even get her shirt back on.

Evil Dead II is ostensibly a remake of the first film. For the sequel, director Sam Raimi incorporated elements of slapstick comedy, taking inspiration from the Three Stooges. The protagonist, Ash Williams, finds himself fending off a horde of demonic Deadites at a secluded cabin in the woods. His right hand becomes possessed by one of the evil spirits, so Ash lops it off with a chainsaw. He later attaches the whirring blade to his stump, turning the power tool into a weaponized prosthetic.

Groovy.

Islamic Sharia law permits punitive amputations. Lose a hand for stealing, lose a foot for repeated offense. This practice still exists today in Iran, Saudi Arabia, Yemen, Afghanistan, Sudan, and northern Nigeria.

Thomas Jefferson proposed a bill to allow for judicial amputations in America, suggesting that those found guilty of rape, sodomy, or polygamy should be punished with castration (for men) or by having a hole cut through the cartilage of their nose (for women). Anyone convicted of maiming another person, be it cutting out their tongue, slicing off their ear, or branding their skin, should be like-wise disfigured.

Did Jefferson consider that his proposed punishment would apply to himself? Might he have willingly offered up his hide in accordance with the law after raping his slave Sally Hemings?

1754 B.C.E. Hammurabi, the sixth Babylonian king, codifies the law of retaliation, lex talionis—an eye for an eye, a tooth for a tooth.

The plot of the film *In a Glass Cage* takes a turn with the arrival of Angelo, one of Klaus's former victims. Angelo is hired as a live-in nurse and caretaker for Klaus. His plans for revenge soon become apparent. He murders Klaus's wife and assumes control of the house. He begins reenacting Klaus's crimes, abducting, torturing, and murdering young boys while Klaus watches helplessly from his iron lung.

Disability is like being caught in a trap. You are restrained. Paralyzed. Ensnared within your own flesh. At the same time, you are chained by your fear, frustration, hopelessness, knowing you cannot escape. And the ones who walk free will not release you. No, they will build a cell around you, a trap within a trap.

June 6, 1989. Tsutomu persuades five-year-old Ayako Nomoto to let him photograph her. He takes her to his car and offers her a stick of gum. She comments on his *funny hands.* Tsutomu says, *Here's what happens to kids who say things like that.* He strangles Ayako, wraps her body in a sheet, hides it in the trunk. He brings Ayako to his apartment. He spends two days photographing, filming, and raping her corpse. When the smell becomes noticeable, Tsutomu dismembers Ayako. Her torso he brings to a cemetery; her head he leaves in the hills nearby. Tsutomu keeps her hands, which he later cannibalizes. Fearing the police will discover the remains, Tsutomu retrieves the rotting body parts two weeks later and stores them in his closet.

Odd Nerdrum's painting *Cannibals* shows three figures—a cripple, a madman, a mongoloid—gnawing on the bones and gristle of an unfortunate fourth figure, whose serene face belies his fate. The cannibals wear rags, squatting against a barren apocalyptic wasteland. The cripple's wheelchair appears modern, adding to the temporal disequilibrium. The dead man (or is it a woman?) has been carved up, reduced to a head, spine, and ribcage. The ground is smeared with viscera, organs, blood. Affectless, the cannibals neither enjoy nor recoil at their meal. They have simply satisfied the demands of their biological needs.

Is it evil to follow your nature?

Having developed asthma as a child, Proust had fragile health. Bad digestion, insomnia, cardiac spasms, headaches, back pain, dizziness, gait imbalance, slurred speech, memory loss, thermal dysregulation, and general weakness led to an archaic diagnosis of neurasthenia. He self-medicated with a steady stream of caffeine, sparteine, adrenaline, euvalpine, barbiturates, chloral, ether syrup, morphine, antiasthma cigarettes, pectoral powder fumigations. He experienced episodes of toxic coma at least twice in his life. Toward the end, Proust's diet consisted solely of coffee and cold beer, which he had specially delivered from the Ritz hotel. His condition degenerated into obstructive bronchopneumopathy with superimposed infections, which killed him at age fifty-one.

I call Jill the next day. I know from experience it's better not to wait. Jill answers and I confess. It's over. *I knew you would do this*, she says. *I knew it.* No one is surprised.

Hitchcock. *Rear Window.* Jimmy Stewart as photographer L. B. Jefferies. Broken leg. Stuck in a wheelchair. Heat wave, windows open. Jefferies watching his neighbors. Miss Torso. Miss Lonelyhearts. The manic pianist. The amorous newlyweds. The old couple and their little dog. The sinister Mr. Thorwald, who strangles his wife, chops her up, puts her in a suitcase. Jefferies and his binoculars. Jefferies and his suspicions. Nobody believes him. He needs evidence. Jefferies lures Thorwald out of his apartment and sends his girlfriend Lisa Fremont, played by Grace Kelly. Investigate. Prove. Thorwald back early. Catches

Lisa. Will she be next? No. Here come the police. Lisa carted away in handcuffs. Breaking and entering. But she got what she came for. Evidence. Thorwald locking eyes with Jefferies. He knows. Thorwald confronting Jefferies in the pitch-black apartment. Jefferies with his camera. His only defense. Click. Flash. Click. Flash. Thorwald getting closer. The inevitable struggle. Jefferies thrown out the window. Here come the police again. Just in time to save the day. Just in time to break Jefferies's fall. Just in time to take the cuffs off Lisa and put them on Thorwald. Jefferies back in his wheelchair. Casts on both legs. Still watching his neighbors. Still a voyeur. Still alive.

The 1998 remake of *Rear Window* stars Christopher Reeve in the role of L. B. Jefferies. Unlike Jimmy Stewart, Reeve was an actual cripple. On May 27, 1995, Reeve rode in an equestrian competition with his horse Buck. Preparing to jump a fence, Buck halted, sending Reeve flying forward, hands tangled in the reins. Landing headfirst, Reeve shattered two vertebrae. Instant paralysis. Superman stuck in a wheelchair. No longer mistaken for a bird or a plane. He spent months hooked to a ventilator. After a long regimen of physical therapy, the production of *Rear Window* marked the first time since the accident Reeve was able to breathe without a tube in his neck, albeit only for ninety-minute stretches. The remake was panned.

A horse, a horse, my kingdom for a horse!

The ancient Hindus provided disabled people with special jobs to fit their affliction. Kings employed mute subjects, for instance, to transcribe confidential government documents.

Only 21 percent of disabled Americans are currently employed.

Disabled inmates at Nazi concentration camps were called *Ballastexistenzen*, literally, "ballast existences," dead-weight prisoners. By 1941, commandants began compiling lists of these prisoners for withdrawal from service. Those marked unfit for labor were told they would be transferred to "recovery camps." They were promised medical treatment, lighter duties. Many readily volunteered, only to find themselves carted off to killing centers. Before entering the gas chamber, victims were inspected for gold teeth. Waste not.

January 2009. I'm back in Boston, walking to the dorms from the Amtrak station, dragging my suitcase through the snow. I catch up with everyone, regale them with tales of my drug-induced mayhem. I fall into a routine of staying up all night, sneaking into the Common to smoke since I don't want to get busted indoors again. There's an old wooden bench on a footpath behind a hill deep in the park, a perfectly secluded spot for lighting up. I make fast friends with the security guards who work the graveyard shift, strolling up to the desk red-eyed, my coat reeking, a stupid grin on my wind-chapped face. The guards smile back, a knowing gesture, nodding as I flash my school ID. I watch gory foreign films in my room until the cafeteria opens. I pile my tray with scrambled eggs, sausage, hash browns, toast with butter, orange juice, coffee. Stuffed, I return to my bed and sleep through my classes. My day starts once the sky is dark.

The monster only comes out at night.

While *Freaks* was in production, MGM insisted the film's cast and crew use separate cafeterias during lunch breaks. According to producer Harry Rapf, this measure was taken *so people could get to eat in the commissary without throwing up.*

The cripple invokes disgust because he embodies your frailty, your finitude, your fate. Vomiting, retching, revulsion—these protect you from the defiled body, separate you from the profane, like pulling a blanket over your head to keep the monster away.

Daphne du Maurier wrote the short story that served as the basis of *Don't Look Now.* She had long struggled coming to terms with her sexuality. "Venetian" was her code word for lesbian, and "going to Venice" a euphemism for sex. After the death of her lover Gertrude Lawrence, du Maurier traveled to the literal Venice, hoping to recover from the shock. During this trip, she became frightened after mistaking a dwarf for a child.

If the monster is abject, he is also uncanny. In him we see something strangely familiar, vestiges of his former normalcy, glimpses of a secret reality.

May 12, 1944. All twelve members of the Ovitz family—seven of whom are dwarfs—are deported to Auschwitz. They immediately attract the attention of Dr. Josef Mengele, who has them sequestered to special living quarters for observation. Before the war, the family traveled throughout Eastern Europe, performing music as the Lilliput Troupe. Mengele is uninterested in their song and dance routine. Dwarfs are a rare commodity for the doctor's campaign of human experimentation.

In David Cronenberg's 1986 remake of *The Fly*, an experiment gone wrong has disastrous consequences for Dr. Seth Brundle. While testing a teleportation pod, Brundle's DNA becomes spliced with that of a common housefly. At first the side effects endow Brundle with incredible powers—super strength, agility, libido. But there is a price for playing God. Brundle's body begins to deteriorate. He keeps what pieces he can salvage preserved in jars inside his medicine cabinet. Ears. Fingers. Toes. *Artifacts of a bygone era*, he calls them.

The American photographer Charles Eisenmann is most famous for his portraits of circus and sideshow performers. These so-called monsters of the Gilded Age were immortalized on cabinet cards, a sort of proto-trading-card set. Jojo the Dog-Faced Boy. The Arabian Giant. The Four-Legged Girl from Texas. Chang and Eng the Siamese Twins. The Two-Headed Nightingale. General Tom Thumb. Collect them all.

In no time I'm twenty pounds heavier. I beg Jill to take me back. She knows better, but we give it another try. Late one night at the dorm we're screaming at each other about nothing. The RAs show up. My room has become a popular stop for them. Rebecca takes Jill away. Casey sits down next to me on the bed. *Look, man, I know you two are having some . . . personal problems. We're not trying to pry or anything. We just had to make sure things weren't, ya know, getting violent.* I stop crying, stunned sober. I look Casey in the eyes and ask, *You think I hit her?* He stares at the floor: *I didn't say that. We just have to be sure nobody got hurt.*

Understand? They file a report, another flag on my record. In addition to having a drug charge, I'm labeled emotionally unstable. The whole mess is absurd. I'd never hit a woman. Would I?

The South African athlete Oscar Pistorius became the first double amputee to compete in the Olympic Games. In the summer of 2012, his prosthetic legs carried him into second place during the four-hundred-meter race. Less than a year later, on February 14, 2013, he fired four shots from a 9 mm pistol through the bathroom door of his Pretoria home. Three of the bullets struck and killed his girlfriend, the model Reeva Steenkamp. Pistorius claimed he had mistaken Steenkamp for an intruder and acted in self-defense. The court found otherwise. Pistorius was convicted of murder and sentenced to thirteen years, five months. Happy Valentine's Day.

Fellow double amputee Lisa Bufano says, *I want to be seen as attractive and beautiful and sexy like everyone else. But I think that in my artwork, for me, it's trying to find some comfort with being everything a human can be.*

Have you ever fantasized about fucking a cripple like me? Or does the idea sicken you?

In Peter Greenaway's 1985 film *A Zed & Two Noughts*, twin zoologists Oswald and Oliver Deuce lose their wives in a freak car accident. The driver, a woman named Alba Bewick, survives but has a leg amputated. The twins' grief is infused with morbid scientific curiosity. They become obsessed with photographing decomposing animals, seeking out the very essence of life through decay. Oswald and Oliver also begin a sexual relationship with Alba. A quack doctor convinces Alba to have her other leg amputated. She is perfectly content with her newfound leglessness, concluding that both limbs should complement each other for the sake of symmetry. *Like us*, the twins concur. Alba becomes pregnant and claims that both her lovers will serve as father. When Alba delivers twins, the balance is thrown off. She soon finds another double amputee and names him the father instead. Symmetry restored.

Half of radioulnar synostosis cases are unilateral, affecting only one arm. The other half are bilateral, affecting both arms.

Lucky me.

In Alejandro Jodorowsky's film *El Topo*, the gunslinger duels against a man with no legs strapped to the back of a man with no arms.

If only I could find my opposite—someone whose hands are permanently fixed palm-up.

When she was twenty-three years old, Ellen Stohl became the first disabled model featured in *Playboy*. A car accident left Stohl paralyzed from the neck down. She wrote to Hugh Hefner in the late 1980s, sharing her story and asking to be featured in the magazine. Despite concerns from the editors that the shoot could be misconstrued as exploitative, Hefner agreed to go ahead. Across the eight-page layout, only one photo shows Stohl in her wheelchair (fully clothed). She would later marry, have a daughter, and become a professor of education at Cal State. She posed nude as a means of reconnecting with her own sexuality, to celebrate a part of her stripped away in the accident. Stohl sought to bring together that which our society tries to keep apart: disability and sexuality.

One of the most frequent questions I get is *How do you masturbate?* Man is a resourceful animal. Use your imagination.

Frida and Diego spend a few years traveling the United States. Frida is not a fan. During a stay in Detroit, she becomes pregnant. She fears the injuries sustained during her bus accident will make childbirth impossible. Frida has already undergone an abortion earlier in her marriage. She attempts to have a second abortion, but the procedure fails. On July 4, 1932, Frida miscarries, which causes a serious hemorrhage. She is rushed to the hospital, where doctors terminate the pregnancy. Hospitalized for two weeks, Frida asks to be brought the body of her fetus so she can paint it. Her request is denied.

Disfigured fetuses kept in jars and displayed at sideshows are known as "pickled punks."

A pair of Kahlo's paintings offer surreal versions of her miscarriage. *Henry Ford Hospital* shows Frida lying naked in a bed atop a pool of blood, red ribbons coiling from her belly like umbilical cords, tethering her body to a purple orchid, a pelvis, a snail, a pink orthopedic cast of the female reproductive system, a strange machine, and an enlarged male fetus. *My Birth* depicts a woman on a large bed, a white sheet shrouding her face. Frida's own lifeless head emerges from the womb. A portrait of the Virgin of Sorrows watches over the scene. Frida describes the painting as how she imagined being born.

The ancient Roman Law of the Twelve Tables stated that any child born "dreadfully deformed" should be put to death, typically by stoning.

The Reich Committee for the Scientific Registering of Serious Hereditary and Congenital Illnesses assessed the applications of disabled children selected for the T4 program. Hospitals were required to register any infant born defective. Doctors marked + for death, − for life, and ? for undecided. As the war progressed the screening process became less rigorous, the potential victims older. By 1941, simply being labeled a "juvenile delinquent" was grounds for execution.

Boris Karloff dressed as Santa Claus and handed out presents to disabled children at a Baltimore hospital every year.

I flunk all my classes. The train takes me back home to Maryland. I have no intention of returning to Boston. I call Jill a week later and tell her as much. She asks, *So where does that leave us?* She's crying. I'm not. My voice is calm, flat: *I guess we have to break up.* Jill doesn't take it well. She gave me a second chance, and I threw it back in her face. I know I've hurt her deeply. I don't care.

V

THE DAMNED

September 13, 1848. Cavendish, Vermont. Railroad construction foreman Phineas Gage is directing a work gang, blasting rock to clear a path for the next stretch of track bed. Around 4:30 P.M., Gage looks over his right shoulder and opens his mouth to speak. At the same instant, an explosion sends a tamping iron into Gage's lower jaw and up through the top of his skull. The three feet, seven inches of metal lands eighty feet away. A few minutes later, Gage is speaking, able to walk with some help. An ox cart takes him back to his room in town. The physician Edward H. Williams is dispatched. He finds Gage sitting in a chair outside the hotel, brain matter oozing from his head. Gage says, *Doctor, here is business enough for you.*

In scientific terms, my disability results in restricted inward roll (pronation) and outward roll (supination) of the forearms.

Dr. Josef Mengele makes the normal-sized members of the Ovitz family carry their dwarf siblings to his workshop each day. Searching for signs of hereditary disease, Mengele extracts bone marrow, teeth, hair. He alternates pouring scalding and freezing water into their ears. He blinds their eyes with chemical drops. He instructs gynecologists to examine the women. The youngest Ovitz is eighteen-month-old Shimshon. Mengele takes special interest in the boy. Blood is drawn daily from the child's ears and fingertips. At one point, the family witnesses the execution of two unrelated dwarfs. This unlucky duo have their bodies boiled so the skeletons can be exhibited in museums.

Pliny the Elder describes two giants, a male named Pusio and a female named Secundilla, who both stood nearly ten feet tall. Emperor Augustus assigned these giants to lead his armies into battle, as a means to intimidate the enemy. After death, their skeletons were displayed as decorations in the Gardens of Sallust.

Kristeva says the presence of signified death, like the line of a heart monitor gone flat, is easy for us to accept. Confronted with true abjection—shit, corpses, freaks—the mask is pulled from the horrific essence of life that we all look past in order to carry on. Life barely withstands this defilement—the borderline of the human condition.

We are all here together at the demarcation of life and death, man and monster.

Tsutomu writes a letter to the parents of his first victim, four-year-old Mari Konno. *Before I knew it, the child's corpse had gone rigid. I wanted to cross her hands over her breast but they wouldn't budge . . . Pretty soon, the body gets red spots all over it . . . Big red spots. Like the Hinomaru flag . . . After a while, the body is covered with stretch marks. It was so rigid before, but now it feels like it's full of water. And it smells. How it smells. Like nothing you've ever smelled in this whole wide world.*

Everyone's on summer break. One night Jules and I meet up with Vic at his girlfriend's place by the lake. Cindy is there, the girl who gave us the fateful acid tabs only a few months earlier. I bum her a smoke and we get to talking. I'm good at making her laugh. She's taller than me, with a moon-shaped face and long, straight black hair. She wears thick-framed black glasses and a Sonic Youth shirt, the one with the Raymond Pettibon drawing of the murderous runaway couple. Her sleepy eyes glow behind the cherry as she takes a long drag. The following weekend I invite her to my place. We get high and have sex, and halfway through the bed breaks, spilling us to the floor, where we finish.

Sexuality combines the biological, the physical, the erotic, the emotional, the social. As does disability.

Sexuality is a broad term with myriad definitions and contexts. As is *disability*.

Frida and Diego move to Mexico City in 1934. Frida's health continues to deteriorate. An appendectomy, two more abortions, the amputation of gangrenous toes. The marriage strains. Diego is unhappy living in Mexico and blames Frida for their return. He begins an affair with Frida's younger sister Cristina. Frida counters with an affair of her own, beginning a brief but intense relationship with the Japanese American artist Isamu Noguchi. The couple reconciles by 1935, although both continue their infidelity.

Kathy Bates as the psychotic nurse Annie Wilkes. James Caan as captive novelist Paul Sheldon. Paul driving through Colorado in a snowstorm. Car accident. Two broken legs. Rescued by Annie. Imprisoned by Annie, Paul's number one fan. Demands a rewrite of the latest Misery Chastain book. Paul is Annie's captive. He goes snooping around. Learns about Annie's troubled past. A trail of dead babies. Annie doesn't take kindly to Paul's prying, ties Paul to the bed. Puts a block of wood between his ankles. Breaks both his feet with a sledgehammer. Annie says, *God, I love you.*

Paul's hobbling has historical precedent. Archaeological remains uncovered at the Sacred Ridge site in south-western Colorado show evidence of the practice being employed by ancestral Puebloans more than one thousand years ago, possibly as a means of social control.

Goya's *Beggars Who Get about on Their Own in Bordeaux* is a black-chalk sketch composed sometime between 1824 and 1827. The ghostly figure is pyramid-shaped, sitting mouth agape in his wheelchair, useless legs covered with a blanket. What a luxury to be so independent during such primitive times.

We drive to Rehoboth Beach. My grandmother lends us her vacation house. We take a vodka-filled water bottle to the shore and get drunk lying in the sand. Cindy's wearing jean shorts and a neon-orange tank top over her wet bathing suit. We share french fries on the boardwalk, licking peanut oil and salt off our fingers as seagulls nip at our toes. We wreck go-karts at Fun Land. She uses her fake ID at a liquor store shaped like a giant palm tree. We dance on my grandmother's couch and fall into each other over and over.

Despite his clubfoot, Byron became a notorious Lothario, his sexual exploits now the stuff of legend. There was a scandalous affair with Lady Caroline Lamb, who is famously attributed with describing Byron as *mad, bad, and dangerous to know.* Next came the Lady Oxford. Then Byron's own half sister Augusta Leigh, with whom he was rumored to have fathered a child. A brief marriage with Anne Isabella Milbanke, who in her petition for separation claimed Byron had sodomized her two days after the birth of their daughter Ada. Various flings with Claire Clairmont, stepsister of Mary Shelley. In Venice, there was Marianna Segati, wife of Byron's landlord, as well as Margarita Cogni, wife of an Italian baker. An intense affair with the nineteen-year-old countess Teresa Guiccioli. There was a young housemaid named Lucy with whom he fathered a child. Not to mention a slew of men, including a fourteen-year-old boy from Athens named Nicolo Giraud. And lest we forget Byron's Scottish nanny May Gray, who repeatedly molested the boy from age nine to ten.

A monster with charm is the most frightening of all.

Miraculously, Phineas Gage recovered from the accident. He had lost his left eye and at least an ounce of brain matter. Before the tamping iron passed through his skull, Gage had been described as responsible, hardworking, well liked. His employers called him the most efficient and capable foreman they had ever known.

People change.

After Gage's long convalescence, the physician credited with saving his life, Dr. J. M. Harlow, reported unusual differences in his patient's personality: *He is fitful, irreverent, indulging at times in the grossest profanity (which was not previously his custom), manifesting but little deference for his fellows, impatient of restraint or advice when it conflicts with his desires, at times pertinaciously obstinate, yet capricious and vacillating, devising many plans of future operations, which are no sooner arranged than they are abandoned in turn for others appearing more feasible. A child in his intellectual capacity and manifestations, he has the animal passions of a strong man.*

Becoming a monster is easy.

Lennie Small and his ironic name. Lennie and his dream of living *off the fatta the lan'*. Lennie and his powerful body. Lennie and his feeble mind. Lennie and his dead bunny rabbits. Lennie and his dead puppy dog. Lennie and his boss's dead wife. Lennie and his best friend, George Milton. Lennie and the bullet in his head.

Could you do it? If you had to? Put the beast out of its misery?

HEADLINE NEWS

Phoenix, AZ, 2009. *Torture-Killing of Disabled Man Brings First-Degree Murder Charge; Second Suspect Charged in Dumping of Body.*

Greensburg, PA, 2010. *W. Pa. Man Gets Death in Disabled Woman's Torture.*

St. Louis, MO, 2019. *Woman Gets Life Term in Death of Mentally Disabled Man.*

Chicago, IL, 2020. *Englewood Couple Tortured to Death a Disabled Man Who Paid Them to Help Him, Prosecutors Say.*

Browning, MT, 2020. *Browning Woman Charged with Murder of Disabled Man on Blackfeet Reservation.*

Between 2011 and 2015, at least 219 disabled people were killed by their parents or caregivers in North America, an average of nearly one murder per week. That is a conservative estimate.

Arbus says she adores freaks but wouldn't want to make friends with them. She prefers to maintain a safe distance.

Wanting to photograph cripples is different from enjoying their company.

Cindy is back in Manhattan, studying photography. I stay in Maryland, taking a few classes at a college in town, only a mile from Mom's house. My mind is elsewhere. One night I split a pint of Evan Williams with a girl I know from high school. I kiss her and she laughs. I try to take her belt off and she says, *I'm on my period.* I drive home drunk, piss in the backyard, and slink upstairs, hoping not to wake Mom.

How trite when someone says, *You can do anything if you put your mind to it.*

Charles II of Spain is remembered more for his deformities than his political prowess. The product of inbreeding, Charles endured skeletal abnormalities, epilepsy, intellectual disability, slurred speech, frequent infections, and infertility. Unable to produce an heir, Charles resorted to sleeping beside the disinterred corpse of his father in a superstitious bid to cure impotency.

Dinah Maria Craik's *The Little Lame Prince and His Traveling Cloak* is a parable for children. During his baptism, the infant Prince Dolor is dropped by his nurse, causing paralysis. When the king and queen die, Prince Dolor's evil uncle assumes control. The little lame prince is exiled to a tower in a wasteland. A fairy godmother visits the lonely boy, whose only wish is to walk. Instead, she leaves him a magical cloak that grants him the power of flight.

Professor Xavier using telepathy from his wheelchair. Matthew Murdock leaping from skyscrapers he will never see. Tony Stark with his bum heart weightless in an iron suit. A cripple with superpowers is still a cripple.

French author Blaise Cendrars lost his right arm while serving as a corporal in the Foreign Legion during the First World War. On September 28, 1915, a German shell struck Cendrars while he was stationed in Champagne. With his arm dangling from the bone, Cendrars was loaded onto an ambulance and taken to a nearby nunnery that had been converted into a hospital. Bleeding heavily, Cendrars realized he would die if not soon operated on. He pulled out his pistol and rapped on the operating room's door. When the surgeons answered, he aimed the gun at them and said, *I'm next or I shoot you.* The surgeons complied, amputating Cendrars's right arm and saving his life.

In World War I, military doctors often relied on guillotines to perform quick amputations.

My hands disqualify me from military service. No sense enlisting a cripple if he can't even hold a gun.

Cendrars was offered a prosthetic after his surgery. He refused, becoming affectionately known as the Left-Handed Poet. Cendrars prided himself on being skilled at shooting, driving, typing, boxing—all with one hand. He would go on to publish nearly fifty books in his lifetime.

A majority of amputees experience varying symptoms of phantom limb, the cause of which is not entirely understood.

Cendrars felt phantom pain for the remainder of his life. At the age of seventy, a stroke incapacitated his good arm and hindered his ability to speak. Shortly before his death in 1961, he wrote, *Nothing remains, nothing lasts, except this longstanding pain in my severed arm and this new pain in my intact left arm, which is absolutely astounding in its intensity and unfamiliarity. Enough is enough.*

I ask Cindy if I can visit her for a weekend. She agrees. We set a date. Soon I'm on an early-morning bus heading north on I-95. A few hours later, the bus lets me off near Penn Station. I walk across a crowded thoroughfare. I'm not used to so many people. For a moment I'm sure I'll be lost forever, and then I see her standing on the corner, and she runs at me and jumps and I catch her. She says, *I missed you*, and that's all I need to hear.

Hephaestus, the Greek god of blacksmithing, was born lame, his feet shriveled, useless. Ashamed of her son's ugliness, the goddess Hera exiled Hephaestus from Olympus. He landed on the island of Lemnos, where the Sintian tribe adopted the boy and taught him to become a master craftsman. Seeking revenge on his mother, Hephaestus sent Hera a golden throne outfitted with an invisible trap. When Hera sat on the throne, she found herself unable to stand up again. The other gods begged Hephaestus to free Hera, but he refused, saying, *I have no mother*. Dionysus was sent to retrieve the bitter Hephaestus, getting him drunk on wine until he passed out. Dionysus then carried his crippled cargo back to Olympus strapped atop a mule.

Robert Wyatt spent three months recuperating in a hospital bed after breaking his back. When he was able to get into a wheelchair, Wyatt discovered an old piano in the visitors' room. He began reworking the songs he had started in Venice before the accident. Glad to have something to occupy himself, Wyatt came to view his paralysis as a way to deepen his approach to music. He was free to dream.

Franklin Hardesty is the fourth to die in *The Texas Chain Saw Massacre*. He is the older brother of Sally, lone survivor of the killing spree, the final girl. Throughout the film, Franklin is mocked for his disability. Sally's friends like reminding Franklin of what he cannot do. While exploring the abandoned homestead, he becomes infuriated when he is unable to follow the group up a flight of stairs. Leatherface surprises Franklin in the dark woods. The invalid brother is hacked apart with the titular chainsaw. Hardly a fair fight.

Sometimes I daydream of breaking my wrists with a hammer. Maybe Leatherface will let me borrow his.

Phineas Gage lived another twelve years after the accident. His demeanor normalized with time, but he had trouble holding a job. Epileptic seizures. One of these fits killed him in 1860, aged thirty-six. Among his possessions was the tamping iron that passed through his skull. Dr. Harlow referred to the metal rod as Gage's *constant companion*.

July 26, 2016. Midori Ward, Sagamihara, Kanagawa Prefecture, Japan. Tsukui Lily Garden is a long-term care facility built in a wooded area near the Sagami River. Home to 149 mentally and physically disabled residents between the ages of nineteen and seventy-five. Around

2 A.M., a former employee, Satoshi Uematsu, smashes a first-floor window and breaks into the building. He ties up the staff member on duty and takes his keys. Uematsu proceeds from room to room, methodically stabbing occupants in the neck as they sleep in their beds. In less than an hour, he kills ten people and injures another twenty-six.

Who will survive and what will be left of them?

In letters written to members of the Japanese House of Representatives before the massacre, Uematsu argued in favor of legalizing euthanasia for disabled people. He believed doing so would benefit the economy and prevent World War III. He wrote, *The disabled can only create misery*, and he offered to kill more than four hundred people. Authorities had Uematsu involuntarily committed to a psychiatric hospital. Doctors concluded Uematsu was not a threat so he was released. Four months later he made good on his word.

Cindy takes me to MoMA. We're wandering through the big white rooms, soaking it all in. There's the dead tiger shark floating in a steel tank of formaldehyde. A group of kindergarteners sit cross-legged before Jackson Pollock's *403: Action Painting I* while their teacher stands beside the canvas asking, *How do you think the artist was feeling when he made this?* I find myself frozen in front of Chuck Close's nine-foot-tall painting *Mark*. I'm counting all the pixels. Cindy says, *I'll have my work hanging in here one day*, and I know she's right.

The model for Close's painting, Mark Greenwold, says he never found his portrait shocking or monstrous, despite its size. He did, however, grow a beard after the fact and hasn't shaved it off since.

Frankenstein's monster does not think of himself as a monster until he sees his own reflection in a pool of water.

December 7, 1988. The same year Tsutomu eats his grandfather's ashes, Chuck Close experiences what he calls "The Event." While presenting an award at a ceremony honoring New York City artists, Close feels a strange pain in his chest. Concluding his speech, he walks to the nearby Beth Israel Hospital and suffers a sudden seizure. One of his spinal arteries has collapsed, leaving him paralyzed from the neck down.

The same feeling I had while transfixed by *Mark* at MoMA.

Close regained some mobility through physical therapy but remained wheelchair-bound. He slowly taught himself to paint again, attaching a brush to his wrist with a Velcro strap.

Today the term *wheelchair-bound* is considered outdated and offensive. Disability activists instead recommend *person who uses a wheelchair*.

Ditto for general references to *the disabled*. Even *disabled person* is contentious. Safer to say *person with disabilities*. This way the condition does not supersede the individual. The cripple is not further dehumanized. In theory.

Political correctness is always so dull.

The Wikipedia page "List of Disability-Related Terms with Negative Connotations" has more than one hundred entries.

The last time I speak to my father is on the phone. My sister has just turned eighteen. Dad gives her a guitar. A few days later he asks for the Fender back, explaining that he took it from one of his girlfriend's daughters without permission. I'm seething. I hiss into the mouthpiece: *I know what you did. Lousy fucking prick. Slimeball piece of shit. Your own daughter. On her birthday. I never want to see you again.* We haven't spoken since.

Cripple from the Old English *crypel*, "one who creeps, halts, or limps."

Deformed slaves were prized by the ancient Roman elite and were often purchased for display as a kind of living art. Augustus was known to decorate the rooms of his many villas with these human curiosities, both living and dead. Merchants set up special "monster markets" to meet the incessant demand for anomalous bodies. Plutarch describes witnessing persons *who have no calves, or are weasel-armed, or have three eyes, or ostrich-heads* being regularly bought and sold. Disfigured slaves fetched an even higher price than their able-bodied counterparts because of scarcity. In some cases, slaves were kept in small cages to deliberately stunt their growth—artisanally crafted dwarfs.

MGM hired 124 dwarfs to play Munchkins in *The Wizard of Oz*. Shacked up in the Culver Hotel, the Munchkins were notorious for binge drinking and cavorting with prostitutes, often indulging in wild orgies and getting into violent brawls. Judy Garland claimed she was often groped while filming with the Munchkins and recalled how police would chase the intoxicated Munchkins with butterfly nets.

I'm back working at Wonder Book. One evening I'm ringing up a customer for some paperbacks. He gives me a funny look and says, *Can I ask you a weird question?* I tell him to go ahead. He points: *Noticed your hands. You can't turn them, right?* I nod. He continues, *My brother's got the same thing.* I'm shocked. I've never met another person like me, only heard rumors they exist. I tell the guy to send my regards to his brother. This is the closest I've gotten to shaking the backwards hand of a fellow freak.

A year after his accident, Robert Wyatt scored a surprise hit with a cover of the Monkees' "I'm a Believer." He was booked to perform the song on *Top of the Pops*, but producers were hesitant to let Wyatt appear in a wheelchair on the grounds that it was not suitable for family viewing. Wyatt protested and ultimately won out. In solidarity, Wyatt's backing band all sat in wheelchairs for a cover spread in *New Musical Express*.

Dr. Strangelove grinning maniacally in his wheelchair. Dr. Strangelove wearing one black glove. Dr. Strangelove wrestling with his uncontrollable right hand. Dr. Strangelove giving the Nazi salute. Dr. Strangelove standing up to say, *Mein Führer, I can walk!*

I visit Cindy every few months. We take a trip to Coney Island. Neither of us has ever been. We ride the F train to Neptune Ave. I burn my lips on her one-hitter. We eat hot dogs on the boardwalk. There are no freak shows. We buy tickets for the Wonder Wheel. The little red carriage rocks us 150 feet in the air. I wipe my sweaty palms against my jeans. We watch the skyline, the night haze. We hang there, suspended in time. Her head on my shoulder. The floral smell of her black hair mixes with the salty air. I tell her I'm fed up with just seeing her every couple of months. I tell her I want to drop out of school and quit working at the video store. I tell her I want to move to the city. I have enough money saved up. The little red carriage jerks. The wheel keeps spinning. Down we go.

When he was twelve years old, Joseph Stalin was struck by a horse-drawn carriage. He was seriously injured and hospitalized for several months. Extensive surgery resulted in his left arm becoming significantly shorter than his right and rigid at the elbow. Stalin concealed his disfigurement in official portraits, but little could be done to amend the pain that would trouble him for the remainder of his life.

After returning to Olympus, Hephaestus was given his own palace, complete with a workshop for his blacksmithing.

There he crafted magnificent equipment for the other gods. Winged helmet and sandals for Hermes. The Aegis breastplate for Athena. A girdle for Aphrodite. Armor for Achilles. Chariot for Helios. Bow and arrows for Eros. Hephaestus also forged the first human woman, Pandora, and her infamous box.

Cindy comes down to help me pack for the big move. We rent a minivan. We cross the George Washington Bridge, Lou Reed's "Street Hassle" playing on the stereo. My apartment is in Bed-Stuy, right next to the Marcy Projects and the Crown Fried Chicken where Jay-Z used to hang. On the corner is a mobile police watchtower with tinted windows. I have a sack of clothes, some flimsy plastic dishware, boxes full of books. I don't have a bed. I sleep on the floor. I'm happy.

432 C.E. The Byzantine general Aspar is deployed to northern Africa during a campaign against the Vandals. There he purchases a Moorish dwarf named Zercon, who becomes the general's personal jester. Ten years later the Huns capture Zercon. He is now the property of King Bleda, Attila's older brother. Zercon serves as Bleda's constant companion, until the king is murdered by Attila in a power grab. Not only does Attila inherit the throne; he also gains possession of Zercon.

We represent the Lollipop Guild, the Lollipop Guild, the Lollipop Guild!

Attila comes to loathe Zercon, whose appearance both disgusts and frightens the king. Humped shoulders, twisted feet, flat nose, black skin, lisp.

And on behalf of the Lollipop Guild, we'd like to welcome you to Munchkinland!

Attila pawns Zercon off as a gift to the Roman general Aetius, who eventually returns the dwarf to his original owner, Aspar. Full circle. Until eunuchs assassinate Aspar during an imperial power struggle. Zercon tries to reunite with Attila, but his request is denied. Of the jester's ultimate fate, nothing is known.

Follow the yellow brick road! Follow the yellow brick road!

One thousand five hundred eighty years after Zercon is sold into slavery, the American avant-garde singer-songwriter Scott Walker pens the tune "SDSS1416+13B (Zercon, A Flagpole Sitter)." Twenty-one minutes long, the song follows the doomed jester's attempt to escape the degradation of Attila's court. He ascends through history and time, literally and metaphorically reaching new heights, first as a 1920s-era flagpole sitter and finally as the titular brown dwarf star, slowly dying out, freezing to death in the blackness of deep space.

Meet my roommates: Tess is a call girl who sleeps on the couch. She counts a few NFL players among her clientele, so she says. Ryan is an empty-headed slob who works in a cookie factory. We spend a lot of time getting high and playing his old Super Nintendo. Daquan moves out the day after I move in so he can live with his boyfriend. He sells me his bed for fifty dollars. Phil takes Daquan's place. Phil is an alcoholic chef who comes home one night with blood on his hands. Some junkie sold his girl a bag so Phil beat the shit out of him. I spend most of my time at Cindy's.

Matthew 15:14—*And if the blind guide the blind, both will fall into a pit.*

In the film *Wait Until Dark*, Audrey Hepburn plays the blind housewife Susy Hendrix. She's unaware the doll her husband brings home from the airport is stuffed with heroin. He's keeping it safe for a stranger he met. Good intentions gone bad. The crooks come looking for their dope. Let the gaslighting begin. Poor Susy, so trusting. Until the bodies start piling up. Susy gets wise to the con. Too late. The ruthless Harry Roat, played by Alan Arkin, is coming to collect. Susy kills the lights. Evens the playing field. Until Roat opens the refrigerator, flooding the apartment in cold fluorescence. He doesn't notice Susy has a kitchen knife. Too late. Lights out forever.

Tradition holds that Homer was blind. According to legend, the ghost of Helen grew angry with the poet after he claimed she abandoned her first husband for Alexander. Helen demanded that Homer burn his poems as recompense. He refused. As punishment, Helen robbed him of his sight.

Homer's *Odyssey* tells of Hephaestus's unhappy marriage to the goddess Aphrodite. Repulsed by her husband's lameness, Aphrodite began a long-standing affair with Ares, the god of war. Learning of their tryst, Hephaestus crafted an unbreakable chain-link net and ensnared the lovers while they lay in bed. He hauled them to Mount Olympus, displaying his catch before the other gods, who laughed at the adulterers' shame.

I go with Cindy to meet some friends at an outdoor concert in Chelsea where Twenty-Third Street meets the East River. Andrew W.K. is DJing, wearing all white per usual. Cindy and I split a spliff and drink lukewarm brown-bagged beer. Cold Cave is the headliner. Wesley Eisold wears black leather and dark sunglasses. He's hunched over a synthesizer. Morose darkwave pulses from the stacked amplifiers. Cindy points: *Did you know he only has one hand? Guess he was born that way.* I notice the slack left sleeve. *See?* she asks. *Reminds me of your old girlfriend.*

Having forsaken poetry, Arthur Rimbaud spent his final years traveling between Ethiopia and Yemen, exporting coffee and guns to earn a living. In February 1891, while staying in the port city of Aden, Rimbaud noticed a pain in his right knee. He suspected arthritis. By April the pain had intensified, prompting Rimbaud's return to France for better treatment. Arriving in Marseille in mid-May, he was admitted to the Hôpital de la Conception, where his right leg was amputated.

Les femmes soignent ces féroces infirmes retour des pays chauds.

Doctors offered a grim postoperative diagnosis—bone cancer. Rimbaud spent several months convalescing at his family's farm in Roche before attempting a return to Africa. He didn't get far. Rimbaud found himself once more at the Hôpital de la Conception, where he celebrated his thirty-seventh birthday in excruciating agony. The stump swelled where his leg had been. A tumorous growth sprouted between his hip and stomach. Doctors were impressed at the size. Rimbaud died less than a month later, with his sister Isabelle at his side.

The only way to kill a Deadite in the *Evil Dead* series is total bodily dismemberment.

Lisa Bufano says, *My eye has always been drawn to abnormal forms. It's just that now my tool is my body. I'm still animating a form, but it's my own form. I'm not an astounding dancer. But being a performer with a deformity, I find that there's a gut response in audiences, an attraction/repulsion aspect to it that can be compelling. I just hope that there's a balance between that gut response and the substance of a performance.*

Cindy wants to make a movie. The concept is to cover our bodies in paint. She rents a campus studio and asks her friend to film us. We stand against a plain white backdrop. I strip to my underwear. She does the same. I study the label on a tube of paint: *Is this toxic?* She squirts a glob into her mouth, spits purple in my face. The camera is rolling. We throw handfuls of paint at each other. She rubs silver and blue into my chest. I lick green and gold off her lips. We're drenched, smeared. Paint in our eyes and hair. Paint on our teeth and tongues. We clog the drain in her dorm room shower washing off the mess. I sneak into her school's film lab and edit the footage. We enter our movie into a contest. We don't win.

In Eric Red's 1991 film *Body Parts*, a psychologist named Dr. Bill Chrushank loses his right arm in a horrific car accident. As part of an experimental transplant procedure, Chrushank is given a new limb. He soon begins experiencing visions of murder while losing control of his replacement appendage. Chrushank discovers the arm belonged to notorious serial killer Charley Fletcher, whose limbs have been divvied up to other amputees. One by one, Fletcher—head reattached to a new body— begins collecting his body parts for reassembly, saving Dr. Chrushank for last.

The trope of the sentient severed hand run amok as seen in

The Hand
Idle Hands
The Devil's Hand
The Addams Family
The Beast with Five Fingers
Dr. Terror's House of Horrors
And Now the Screaming Starts!

If I lopped mine off, would they try to kill me?

After the Nazi invasion of Poland on September 1, 1939, the T4 program was expanded to include adults. Throughout the occupied territory, all hospitals and institutions were emptied. Seven thousand disabled Poles shot dead in Danzig. Another ten thousand in Gdynia. Come October, the Nazis switched to carbon monoxide. More efficient. Just before Christmas, Heinrich Himmler personally witnessed one of the gassings. He was happy with the new technology, enough to employ similar methods on millions upon millions of Jews and other non-Aryans.

I get a job at the DVD Funhouse. I work in the basement, listing bootleg DVDs for sale online. When I clock out, I meet Cindy and we pick up tallboy cans and junk food. We get high in her shared bathroom, shower running to dissipate the smoke. We watch the trashiest reality television. Sometimes we meet up with her friends, all of whom I want to sleep with. We go to clubs and yell at each other over the deafening music and buy overpriced mixed drinks. I use a fake ID. The guy's photo bears little resemblance to me, but it always works. The name on the card is Avery. I memorize his birthday for when the bouncers ask. I am not myself.

August 21, 1940. The exiled revolutionary Leon Trotsky is assassinated in Coyoacán. Ice axe to the head. Frida is briefly suspected of involvement, having housed Trotsky for several years at La Casa Azul, where the two also had an affair. A month after she is cleared, Frida travels to San Francisco for medical treatment. Her back pain is flaring up again, not to mention the chronic fungal infection on her hand, both of which are exacerbated by Frida's heavy drinking.

Frida says, *I drank because I wanted to drown my sorrows, but now the damned things have learned to swim.*

Cindy brings me to a party at some art school kid's apartment. I don't know anyone. I sit on the couch drinking beer until Cindy says we should leave to go to some other art school kid's apartment. I have to piss bad when we get outside. I stop in an alley and relieve myself by some trash cans. Before I can finish, a pair of pigs grab me from behind. The meatheads drag me to their cruiser and snatch my license: *They piss on the streets in Maryland?* I get a ticket, a date scribbled on the dotted line. Three months later I show up at the courthouse. I hand my slip to the miserable graying clerk sitting behind a sheet of bulletproof glass. He gives me a number and ushers me into the courtroom. I'm the only white boy. Aside from the judge. And the public defender. I wait until a guard calls my name. I stand next to the lawyer. *What's your charge?* I explain my

situation. He tells me the maximum penalty for public uri-
nation is registry on the sex offender list. The judge asks
if I have a medical condition. I say, *No, your honor, it was just
a stupid mistake.* He issues me a fifty-dollar fine. Cindy is
waiting outside: *Should've held it like I told you.*

The first section of Roberto Bolaño's final novel *2666*,
"The Part about the Critics," follows four academics
who have built their careers around studying the elusive
German writer Benno von Archimboldi. Attempting to
locate the mysterious author, three of the critics travel
to Mexico. They engage in a tempestuous love triangle
until the lone woman of the group, Norton, abandons her
able-bodied colleagues and commits to a relationship with
the sole critic who remained in Europe, a crippled Italian
scholar.

Roberto Bolaño died at the age of fifty after a prolonged
illness resulted in liver failure. At the time of his death in
2003, he was third on the waitlist for a liver transplant.

Shall we count the infinite number of ways the body
betrays itself?

Kristeva says that for the body to become truly symbolic, it
must be clean, proper, with no remnant of its debt to nature.

My hands. My debt.

Tsutomu drank blood from his final victim's severed hands. Little five-year-old hands.

Tell me, where is the symbolism there?

Life in Bed-Stuy is restive. Someone breaks into our apartment but leaves empty-handed. We don't have anything worth stealing. A man is shot in the head at the end of our block. One night our upstairs neighbor comes down to visit. He shows us a computer program on his laptop that translates brain waves into music. He hooks Phil up to some electrodes and strange sounds emerge from the tinny speakers. The upstairs neighbor is complaining about his roommate's personal hygiene. *F' real, this dude smells like dookie,* he says. *Probably don't wipe his ass right. Probably goes from his ass crack to his balls. F' real, people be wiping from back to front is nasty.* Everyone agrees. I don't tell him how I have to wipe this way because of my hands. I don't want him to know how nasty I am.

ADA-compliant restrooms require that access to the sink be thirty by forty-eight inches, and clearance between the side and rear of the stall, sixty by fifty-six inches, with the toilet located sixteen to eighteen inches from the side wall at a height of seventeen to nineteen inches.

Have you ever permitted yourself the luxury of using a handicap stall? No sense letting all that legroom go to waste.

I meet Cindy and her friends at the Double Down. The only light comes from TV sets mounted into the walls playing hardcore BDSM pornography. Ropes, whips, hot wax. We order the house special—rail whiskey with a tall-boy PBR and a Twinkie on the side. Nestled in a corner booth, I sit across from Glenda. She's an English major who wears only black and has the side of her head shaved. We discuss magical realism and Márquez. Glenda leans across the table and shouts over the punk music spewing from the jukebox: *I loved your new piece.* I've been writing essays for a blog run by some ex-*VICE* dirtbags. I thank her for the compliment. She puts her mouth next to my ear: *I've read everything you've written.* After last call I ask Glenda if I can crash on her couch to skip the trek back to Brooklyn. Walking along Delancey, Cindy tells me not to do anything stupid before breaking off from the group to go back to her dorm. Glenda gets me high, and we watch a nature documentary about fire ants. We don't do anything stupid, but I certainly consider it.

Segregated work environments for disabled persons are known as "sheltered workshops." There cripples are provided with menial jobs. Slapping labels on jars. Stuffing envelopes. Greeting customers. This type of work is often described as the "eight F's"—food, fetching, folding, filing, flower, festive, friendly, and filth.

An estimated 420,000 disabled workers in America receive an average wage of $2.15 per hour. This exploitation is courtesy of a loophole in the Fair Labor Standards Act. Wages may be paid out on the basis of productivity or ability, sometimes at a rate as low as three cents per hour. Employers justify such wages through claims of charity. They're giving jobs to people who would never otherwise find one.

On a bitter November night I drink a sixer by myself before catching the J train into Manhattan. I meet Cindy at Kip's place. Kip and I are buddies from back home, went to school together, partied together, worked at Wonder Book together. Difference is he got into NYU and I didn't. Plus, his parents pay for his St. Mark's loft, whereas I can barely scrounge enough working full-time to live in a Bed-Stuy rat hole. I'm swaying when I walk up the three flights and through Kip's door. A whole bunch of us go to some club, where we have to wait in line before the doormen let us in.

A few whiskey gingers erase my mind. I break a glass and am promptly bounced. None of my friends seems to notice, not even Cindy. She won't answer her phone. I leave her a voice mail. *Thanks for abandoning me—fucking bitch,* I hiss before hanging up. I tumble into a subway stop. It's late and the trains are running far apart. I lean against the cool white tiled wall and slide down until I'm sitting on the ground. Across the platform a man without arms plays a trumpet with his toes. I want to toss him some change, but he seems miles away. Finally the train comes, and I go back across the water and puke on the sidewalk and pass out in my secondhand bed, dreamless.

Four women have accused the artist Chuck Close of sexual misconduct. The actress Julia Fox was invited to model for Close in October 2013. When she arrived at his Manhattan studio on Bond Street, Fox was asked to undress. She reluctantly complied, despite no prior discussion of posing nude. Close wheeled himself over to Fox, his face parallel with her groin, and said, *Your pussy looks delicious.* Fox immediately dressed and left the studio, but not before Close offered to pay her two hundred dollars, which she refused.

Cindy is at her internship. I have a rare day to myself. A rare day when I don't have to pretend everything is fine.

I check out the Gysin retrospective at the New Museum, a short walk from Cindy's dorm. I pore over the collages. The cut-ups. *Calligraffiti of Fire.* Letters. Diaries. I study Burroughs's handwriting. There's a small room off to the side. I sit in the darkness, eyes closed. The Dream Machine activates. At its center is a single bare bulb. Rotating rapidly around it is something like a lampshade with pieces cut out. The flickering light and ever-changing patterns are meant to induce hallucinations. I stay for a long time. I feel nothing.

Charles Sherwood Stratton, better known as General Tom Thumb, stood only three feet, three inches tall. He achieved great fame touring with P. T. Barnum in the 1840s and was handsomely compensated for his services—$150 a week, more than $4,000 in today's currency. By the time he retired, he lived in a wealthy Manhattan neighborhood, wore only the finest clothes, and owned a private yacht.

In the *Leprechaun* films, Warwick Davis plays the evil leprechaun Lubdan. Standing three feet six inches tall. Killing anyone foolish enough to steal his precious gold. In space. In the hood. More than forty victims across six franchise installments. Talk about not letting a disability limit oneself.

Werner Herzog's 1970 film *Even Dwarfs Started Small* follows a group of dwarfs institutionalized on a small island who rebel against the hospital staff (also dwarfs). During production, one of the actors was run over by a van but sustained no injuries. The same actor then caught fire while filming another scene. Herzog managed to beat out the flames, leaving the actor mostly unscathed. Herzog made a bet with the crew. If no more accidents occurred, the director would let the actors film him jumping into a cactus patch. When the shoot wrapped without further incident, Herzog made good on his word. He later remarked that *getting out was a lot more difficult than jumping in.*

January 27, 1945. The Red Army liberates Auschwitz. Among the survivors are the Ovitz dwarfs. They are taken to a refugee camp in the Soviet Union before resettling in Israel, where they continue touring and performing for large crowds.

The original tagline for *Freaks*: *Can a full grown woman truly love a midget?*

Perla Ovitz believes God made her a dwarf to save her life, for if Perla had been born a healthy girl of normal height, the Nazis would have found no use for her.

After almost a year in the city I ask Cindy if we can get a place together when she graduates. She prefers not to. This is the death blow. I ask her why not, and she says, *I need to focus on my career.* She had made her choice long before, and I'm just now realizing I'll always be second place. She's a brilliant artist, married to her work. She belongs here. I don't. I quit my job at the DVD Funhouse. I ask my landlord for the security deposit, and he laughs and tells me I've got two weeks to get the fuck out. I call Mom and she rents a U-Haul. I spend a final night with Cindy. We have sex, but it doesn't feel good. We're crying. Neither of us can believe this is happening. The next day I'm back in Maryland finishing a twelve-pack in Mom's basement, punching the concrete floor until my knuckles split.

VI

TERROR IS A MAN

I drive up backroads into the watershed. I park at Nathaniel's Place, the little outcrop dedicated to some kid who hanged himself. I walk down the overgrown trail. There used to be a cabin in the clearing. Its stone chimney is the only piece left. When I step out of the brush, I see a charred fire pit, empty beer cans, junk food wrappers. The old chimney has been smashed to pieces. I nudge the pile of bricks with my foot. I stand at the cliff and study the gurgling stream below. I sit on the edge staring down. I spit and watch the loogie plummet. Plop. It would be easy.

My father found his girlfriend's husband's body in a parking garage. Shotgun. My father and his girlfriend broke up not long after.

I've often thought about the best way to do it. Razor. Painkillers. Noose. Car. Jump. Drown. Gun. But I always find an excuse. Not quick enough. Unpractical. Too messy.

Richard Widmark plays the psychotic gangster Tommy Udo in *Kiss of Death*. He's hired to kill another crook, Pete Rizzo. When he shows up at the target's apartment, Tommy finds only Rizzo's crippled mother. *Where's that squealin' son of yours?* he asks. Mama won't talk. Tommy ties her up with an electrical cord—naturally. Tommy's laughing. Pushes her and her wheelchair right out of the apartment. Right down the stairs.

The modern stair lift was created in the 1920s by self-taught engineer C. C. Crispen. He built the lift, originally called the Inclin-ator, to help an ailing friend. Historians have traced the invention of a similar device back to the sixteenth century. After a jousting accident, King Henry VIII relied on a chair attached to a block and tackle system. Servants dutifully hauled the four-hundred-pound monarch up and down the stairs of Whitehall Palace, often several times a day.

In Jim Thompson's novel *Savage Night*, a diminutive hit man named Charlie "Little" Bigger poses as a college student in the small town of Peardale on the orders of a mafia boss known only as the Man. Charlie moves into a ramshackle boardinghouse run by his intended target—a snitch set to testify for the feds in court. A vicious womanizer, Charlie becomes fixated on the live-in maid. Ruthie appears to have only one leg and uses a crutch to hop from room to room. When Charlie seduces her, he discovers an underdeveloped appendage beneath Ruthie's dress, what Charlie describes as her *baby leg*.

Charlie says that limping around on the crutch has done wonders for Ruthie's rear end, comparing it to that of a Shetland pony.

After the rat is dispatched, Charlie and Ruthie skip town and hide out in an abandoned farmhouse. Ruthie gets stronger and stronger. Her baby leg starts to grow. Soon enough she's able to ditch the crutch. Terrified of this cripple turned femme fatale, Charlie hides in the cellar, certain that Ruthie has been working for the Man since the beginning, an insurance policy in case he botched the job. Charlie's mind starts to slip in the dark underground. Has he imagined everything? Charlie risks a peek out of the cellar's trap door and finds Ruthie waiting with an axe.

I hate to complain. I could have it worse. At least I can walk.

The 1988 film *Mac and Me* is a wonderfully bad *E.T.* knockoff. Its most infamous sequence features a crippled boy named Eric chasing after an alien, Mac. Eric loses control of his wheelchair on a hill and goes flying off a cliff into a lake, where he almost drowns. At the end, Eric is killed during a shootout with police. Mac uses his extra-terrestrial powers to resurrect Eric but stops short of fixing the boy's legs.

Spina bifida is Latin for "split spine."

Jade Calegory, who played Eric, was born with spina bifida and uses a wheelchair in real life. He had his first surgery at eight months old and would undergo another fourteen procedures before his screen debut. While doing publicity for the film and tiring of reporters always asking how he ended up in a wheelchair, Jade took to replying straight-faced: *Vietnam.*

My new girlfriend is my old girlfriend's best friend. Bailey is like me, coming out of a bad breakup. She has big eyes and round cheeks, her pale skin covered with tattoos. A Sal-vador Dalí elephant on her forearm. An outline of the state of Maryland behind her ear. I've had a secret crush on her since high school. Now we're official. We turn twenty-one together. She's living in an apartment outside of Baltimore. We deflate her air mattress. Our friends call it a rebound. I tell Bailey I love her, and I mean it. After a few months we get tired of driving the hour back and forth.

There goes Divine pushing around Mary Vivian Pearce in a stolen wheelchair after running her down with a red '59 Cadillac El Dorado convertible.

We rent a room in Frederick. Our roommate, Adrian, is an alcoholic who works in IT. We decide to move out after only a few months. Adrian says we have to pay him for the rest of the year. We never signed a lease, so I tell Adrian he's not getting another fucking dime. He leaps off the couch, knocking over his collection of spent Stella Artois bottles, gets right in my face, screaming he's going to kill me. I don't flinch. *Go ahead,* I say, *put your hands on me. Then I can take your ass to court for assault and battery. Maybe you'll go to jail. I'm sure you'll lose that nice job you've got. How's that sound?* He slinks to his room. The next morning while Adrian is at work, Bailey and I move everything to Mom's house. By midday the apartment is nearly bare. Most of the furniture is ours. We don't leave a note. We never see Adrian again. Bailey laughs: *How's he going to eat without a microwave?*

April 15, 2007. West Seattle. Brian Sheridan Walsh is drinking with his developmentally disabled roommate Harold "Benny" Reside. Tempers flare. Walsh gets angry. Calls Reside a drain on the welfare system. Walsh starts beating Reside, who is trapped in a wheelchair. When police arrive, Reside is no more. He's been strangled with an electrical cord and cut with pieces of broken ceramic. Walsh gets eighteen years in prison—just another drain on the system.

At what point does a life become worthless?

In the 1942 Nazi propaganda film *Dasein ohne Leben— Psychiatrie und Menschlichkeit* (*Existence without Life: Psychiatry and Humanity*), a group of inmates at a euthanasia center are described as *crippled in body and soul, miserable wretches, a burden to both themselves and to others, like ghosts without a will, imagination, or feeling.*

A trait the Nazis did not lack—imagination.

Hob Broun's short-story collection *Cardinal Numbers*, which was written following his paralysis, contains this line: *modus operandi: montage, collage, bricolage.*

Remind you of anything you've read recently?

I start working in a café, and Bailey gets a job at a dive bar. I wake up at five every morning and spend the next eight hours brewing coffee, toasting bagels, busing tables. I come home smelling like milk and tuna fish. Eventually we save up enough money and find an apartment of our own, no roommates. The hundred-year-old building is next to a church downtown. Go up three flights of stairs to the top, and there it is, a tiny one bedroom with high ceilings and big windows and lots of light. Somehow we haul everything up the narrow, winding staircase. We assemble a shitty IKEA bed and argue over the directions. We're happy.

The Ashtavakra Gita says that if you want to be free, you must set aside your body and sit within total self-awareness.

Admitting to your limitations can be liberating. Or devastating. To say: *I can't do it. I never will.* Then what?

Some dwell on what will never be. Others move on to different realms of possibility. Some become saints. Others become monsters.

Two choices. Two hands.

In the first year of our relationship, Bailey acquires a stalker. He is a customer where she works. The stalker memorizes Bailey's schedule. He sits at a table and watches her from across the room. He asks her out and she declines, and he asks again. When Bailey switches her shifts around, the stalker calls to check if she's there. He follows her in his car. She loses him on the highway. Bailey endures months of this. I buy her a tube of mace. The stalker doesn't relent. Bailey quits her job.

The monster always stalks his victim before the kill. He loves to see them run. He relishes the chase, the pursuit. The monster takes his time, savors the hunt. As prey, the monster seeks out his opposite. The young. The beautiful. The healthy. No sport in chasing fellow cripples.

Between 1940 and 1954, Frida is prescribed a succession of twenty-eight different orthopedic corsets to aid her failing spine. One steel, three leather, the rest plaster. She describes these treatments as *punishment*. At one point, she spends three months in a nearly vertical position with bags of sand tied to her feet in an attempt to straighten her spinal column. Frequently confined to a bed, Frida begins painting her corsets, adorning the front pieces with a red hammer and sickle, shooting stars, a sleeping fetus.

The 2015 horror-western film *Bone Tomahawk* follows a group of frontiersmen battling a cannibalistic tribe of Native American mutant "troglodytes." While escaping from the cannibals' cave, the settlers notice two pregnant troglodyte women lying on a stone slab, blinded with wooden pegs through their eyes, limbs amputated.

Harvard biologist Charles Davenport defined eugenics as *the science of the improvement of the human race by better breeding.*

I get cast in a stage adaptation of *A Clockwork Orange.* I'm a droog, one of the roving gang members. The pack of us tears across the stage, fighting and stomping and bleeding and killing and raping and singing. One night, just before intermission, an audience member walks out. We joke about it backstage, figuring he must've been offended by the violence and depravity. But no, we learn later from the ushers that the man was upset because the play, written by Anthony Burgess himself, was different from the film.

In Kubrick's version, the gang leader Alex is cured of his violent impulses through the Ludovico technique, an experimental form of aversion therapy. Freed from incarceration, Alex lands in the care of Mr. Alexander, a writer whom Alex savagely attacked during the infamous "Singin' in the Rain" sequence. Now in a wheelchair, Mr. Alexander exacts his revenge by playing Beethoven's Ninth Symphony, which triggers Alex's conditioning and drives him to leap out a window in a desperate attempt to escape the pain. Cripples can be notoriously spiteful.

Blessed Margaret of Castello was born to a family of Italian nobles. She was also born a blind, lame, hunchbacked dwarf. Ashamed of their offspring's appearance, Margaret's parents kept her imprisoned for fourteen years. In 1303 Margaret was brought to a shrine in Castello, where her parents hoped for a divine cure. When God granted no such miracle, Margaret's parents abandoned her on the spot. Adopted by nuns, she went on to found a religious school and was admitted to the Third Order of St. Dominic. Upon her death, the townspeople demanded that Margaret be entombed at the local church. The priest protested, but after a crippled girl was miraculously cured at the funeral, he relented.

Sanctuary! Sanctuary!

I text Cindy. We haven't spoken in three years. We pick up where we left off as if nothing happened. We flirt, fawn over the past. Bailey sees the messages on my phone. Of course she does. I sleep on the couch for a week until Bailey forgives me. I text Cindy again. Of course I do. Bailey finds out again. Of course. I'm back on the couch. We're screaming at each other. I grab her shoulders: *Is this what you want? Is this what you want?* She shoves me backwards and I crash into the closet. The door never closes the right way again.

Less than three weeks before her murder, Reeva Steenkamp messaged Oscar Pistorius: *I'm scared of you sometimes, of how you snap at me.*

Fear, the monster's currency.

Surveys suggest that around two-thirds of the able-bodied population feel uncomfortable around disabled persons.

Why shouldn't they? The disabled body encompasses loss, pain, suffering, disorder, death. How could you not be afraid?

Monster, from the Latin *monstrum*, "a divine omen indicating misfortune," derivative of *monere*, "to remind, warn, foretell."

The monster reminds us of our awful potential.

In the Western literary canon, Grendel is the prototypical monster. There have been countless depictions of Grendel on-screen and off, usually as a hulking beast. The original author of *Beowulf*, though, offers no concrete description of Grendel (or his mother) in the source text. We know he is a descendant of the biblical Cain. We know he is a *scea-dugenga*, a shadow walker. We know he eats men. We know that, despite his ferocity, he is something of a mama's boy. Would it be fair to call Grendel disabled? Certainly—at least after Beowulf yanks off the poor creature's arm.

I atone. Delete Cindy's number from my phone. Let Bailey check my messages when she asks. I don't know why she stays with me. A friend tells me Cindy has started seeing someone, another artist, a woman. *Switched teams* is the phrase my friend uses. *They're performing with Grimes*, my friend tells me. They make an avant-garde film together. They tour the country. They're internet famous. All my premonitions are coming true. I pretend not to be jealous.

Why does Cain slay his brother Abel? The book of Genesis does not tell us. The commonplace assumption is jealousy. It's simple: Abel was righteous, Cain evil. God curses Cain for his sins. A mark. A blemish. A defect. A visible sign to let the world know. Something is wrong with that one. Just look at him.

At age fifty-five, the Argentinean writer Jorge Luis Borges went completely blind. His condition was a sort of family curse. Borges's father, grandfather, and great-grandfather all died blind. Still, he continued to write, or rather, dictate, for the latter half of his life, never bothering to learn braille. He embraced the dark. *For the task of an artist, blindness is not a total misfortune. It may be an instrument.*

Ancient Romans highly regarded blindness, believing it bestowed the gift of foresight.

I encounter a blind man on my way to work. He's old but fit. Dark, rectangular sunglasses. No cane. He stands on the curb listening for cars. I ask if he needs help crossing the street. He shakes his head and walks into traffic. A big black SUV brakes, horn blaring. The blind man makes it to the other side and disappears into a sandwich shop. I admire the blind man's cavalier manner. What you can't see can't hurt you, right?

Fede Álvarez's 2016 film *Don't Breathe* tells the story of three petty criminals who rob houses in Detroit. On a tip from their fence, they decide to burglarize the home of a blind Gulf War vet who is rumored to have $300,000 in cash. The blind man proves more formidable than expected, trapping the trio in his house and picking them off one by one. But not before they discover a pregnant woman being held captive in the basement.

There's always a twist. Except when it comes to my wrists.

Mom remarries after being single for almost twenty years. Ken is her high school sweetheart. He's a quiet, kind man. My sister and I are happy for them. His three kids don't much care for us. We don't mind. At the ceremony, I'm a few drinks in when my Nona's latest husband limps to my side. Melvin starts his usual guilt-trip routine: *You need to call your grandmother more.* I do not respond well to his lecture. While Mom and Ken are popping a bottle of champagne, I come close to kicking away Melvin's cane and laying him on his ass. Bailey pulls me away, cools me off. I keep drinking until the old toad is off my mind.

June 1945. Frida flies to New York City seeking relief. Her back pain has worsened. Surgeons extract a piece of bone from her pelvis and fuse it with four of Frida's vertebrae alongside a fifteen-centimeter metal rod. The results are mixed. A few months later the pain returns, intensifies. Frida is ordered to lead a quiet life with frequent rests. She does not listen. Back in Mexico, a fresh batch of doctors scrutinizes the aftermath. They determine that the boys in New York bungled the procedure, grafted the wrong spot. Frida does her body no favors when, in a fit of rage, she reopens the fresh wounds. Doctors advise against painting. Frida will not hear it. There are masterpieces to be made.

Hard to admit you're a cripple. Harder still to admit you're a monster.

Bailey answers her phone. She collapses to the floor. She wails. She covers her mouth with her hand. I stand in the living room of our little apartment on the top floor of the old building next to the church on a quiet street downtown. Bailey drops the phone and sobs. I crouch beside her: *What's wrong?* She cries for a long time. *Michael,* she says. *Michael. Michael. Michael.*

The most prevalent reason for assisted suicide requests within the disabled community is not pain relief but a perceived lack of care and support services. State-sanctioned euthanasia is cheaper than the cost of providing long-term treatment.

Michael is Bailey's friend from Baltimore. I know him as a young, exuberant Black gay man who laughs and dances and makes the people around him do the same. When his boyfriend walks out on him, Michael goes to the top of their apartment building. He jumps.

Why does the monster choose to hurt others instead of himself? If his own shape disgusts him so much, why not do away with it? He is selfish, petty. He wants others to suffer as he suffers. He wants you to share his misery, his pain. The monster joys in the power he wields. To terrorize, to hunt, to kill.

Louis Creed, the protagonist of Stephen King's 1983 novel *Pet Sematary*, moves to a large house in rural Maine with his wife and two young children. Creed's wife, Rachel, is uncomfortable discussing the subject of death. Too bad she's a character in a book about reanimated corpses. Rachel was traumatized at an early age after witnessing the death of her sister Zelda, who was born with spinal meningitis. Forced to care for her hideously disfigured sibling, Rachel routinely feeds the bedridden Zelda. One day while their parents are out, Zelda chokes on her food, expires. Rachel runs for help. The neighbors find the little girl crying. Later, Rachel admits she was laughing, ecstatic to be free of her burden, this waste, this curse.

Mentally dead . . . human ballast . . . empty shells of human beings—Nazi doctors described people with disabilities as.

Robert Frost, W. Somerset Maugham, and Sherwood Anderson were all members of the Euthanasia Society of America.

I get cast as Tom Wingfield in a production of *The Glass Menagerie*. Like Tom, I am twenty-three, restless, fatherless, with dreams of being a famous writer. On the stage, my mother's twin sister plays my mother, the fading Southern belle Amanda Wingfield. I memorize the long, winding monologues and speak directly to the audience. Each night I look these strangers in the eyes and recall Tom's memories as if they were my own. On good nights, tears streak my cheeks when I say the last line: *And so goodbye.*

Tennessee Williams's older sister, Rose, inspired the character Laura Wingfield, a disabled recluse whose only solace is her collection of glass animals. Rose had schizophrenia. The year before Williams's memory play garnered him fame and fortune, Rose was subjected to a botched lobotomy and had to be institutionalized for the remainder of her life. Williams used the royalties from *Summer and Smoke* to arrange for Rose's care in a private sanatorium, where she lived until her death in 1996, outliving her younger brother by nearly a decade.

The solution of the problem of the mentally ill becomes easy if one eliminates these people, quipped an SS officer during a national meeting of leading government psychiatrists and administrators.

We are so easy to erase. The cripple is dispensable. Pretend we don't exist. Keep telling yourself, like monsters— there's no such thing.

July 23, 1989. A Sunday. The City of Hachioji. Two sisters play near a public fountain. Tsutomu stops his car and approaches the girls on foot. *You stay here*, he tells the elder sister, before escorting the youngest toward a nearby river. Big sister runs to get their father. He finds the little sister naked. Tsutomu is trying to insert the zoom lens of his camera into the girl's vagina. The father grabs Tsutomu, throttles him to the ground. Tsutomu slips away, heading for the river's swampy edge.

The café where I work is near a school for the deaf. I'm the only employee in the shop from 6 to 7 A.M. A deaf woman comes in before sunrise. She writes what she wants on a sticky note and hands it to me. Big order. I ring her up and get the drinks going, and while the espresso brews, I start toasting her bagels. Five minutes later I've got the breakfast sandwiches all bagged and the drinks tucked snugly in a cardboard holder. When the deaf woman takes her haul, she doesn't leave a tip. Instead, she passes me another sticky note before hurrying out the door. *You need to work on your multitasking.* I crumple the paper and throw it in the trash.

Disability does not preclude one from being an asshole. I should know.

In Anthony Waller's 1995 film *Mute Witness*, a deaf special-effects makeup artist named Billy unwittingly observes the production of a snuff film. While working on a low-budget slasher movie, Billy gets locked in the studio overnight. She discovers a clandestine crew shooting what appears to be a porno. That is, until the blood starts flowing. Billy soon becomes the next target. If only they could've talked out their differences.

Plato offers an early written account of sign language in *Cratylus*. While discussing the relationship between names and objects, Socrates asks, *If we hadn't a voice or a tongue, and wanted to express things to one another, wouldn't we try to make signs by moving our hands, head, and the rest of our body, just as dumb people do at present?*

I get cast as John Merrick in a production of Bernard Pomerance's *The Elephant Man*. My third dramatic role as a fellow cripple. The play famously eschews the use of makeup or prosthetics. I manipulate my body to portray Merrick's deformities. I bend and twist my spine, hoist one shoulder higher than the other, curl my right arm into a useless thing, contort my face. Drool spills from my clenched mouth. I inflect my voice to sound British, bump my pitch an octave—childlike. I walk with a cane, hobbling across the stage. I build a model of St. Philip's Church. I fall in love with an actress playing an actress. Every night I kill myself by lying down flat, asphyxiated by the weight of my own enormous head. Applause.

Ladies and gentlemen . . . brace yourselves up to witness one who is probably the most remarkable human being ever to draw the breath of life.

The character John Merrick is based on the real-life Joseph Merrick, born August 5, 1862, in Leicester. When he first began exhibiting signs of physical deformities, Merrick's family told the boy his symptoms were the result of his mother Mary being knocked over by a fairground elephant while she was pregnant. Maternal impression. Merrick's left side appeared fairly normal, but the right half of his body ballooned to nightmarish proportions. The deformities made it nearly impossible for him to find work. He tried rolling cigars until his right hand became inoperative. He tried hawking for a haberdashery shop but was met with frequent hostility as he limped from door to door. Deformed lips rendered his speech unintelligible. He was both a curiosity and a horror. After his mother died, the relationship between Merrick and his father soured. Unable to earn any money and loathed by his stepmother, Merrick was treated as a burden to the family. A particularly severe beating from his father convinced Merrick it was time to leave home. He ended up in a workhouse in the winter of 1879. Joseph Merrick was seventeen years old.

Sorting out their new wards, workhouse authorities designated Merrick as "Class One," an able-bodied male.

Four years in the workhouse. Four years in hell. Merrick plotted his escape. He solicited the aid of a local music-hall proprietor named Sam Torr. Merrick offered his services for a human novelty exhibition, as freak shows were a popular attraction at the time. Merrick was billed as the Elephant Man. Half man, half elephant. Torr eventually passed Merrick off to the showman Tom Norman, who ran penny gaffs in London. By November 1884, Merrick found himself in the East End, displayed in the back of a shop in Whitechapel, the same neighborhood Jack the Ripper prowled.

To see actors perform in a play or freaks perform in a sideshow, you buy a ticket all the same.

The shop where Merrick was exhibited sat across from London Hospital. A prominent surgeon, Frederick Treves, inevitably made Merrick's acquaintance and brought him in for an examination. His reaction was less than sympathetic. Treves called Merrick *the most disgusting specimen of humanity that I had ever seen . . . at no time had I met with such a degraded or perverted version of a human being as this lone figure displayed.*

Imagine how I felt on stage, standing in front of a hundred people in nothing but my underpants.

As freak shows fell out of fashion in London, Merrick was sent abroad for a tour of continental Europe. In Brussels, Merrick was robbed and abandoned by his new manager. He secured passage back to England but found himself stranded at Liverpool Street Station. He begged for help. No one could understand his garbled speech. A crowd soon gathered around the exhausted and delirious Merrick. Police were dispatched, though they too could make no sense of what the Elephant Man was saying. Their only clue was a calling card found in Merrick's pocket—Dr. Frederick Treves.

A man in the heyday of youth who was so vilely deformed that everyone he met confronted him with a look of horror and disgust, Treves described Merrick as.

Treves admitted Merrick to London Hospital. The case of the Elephant Man had garnered much public attention, and a slew of donations made it possible for Merrick to be provided with permanent lodgings in the hospital's basement. Per Treves's instructions, the room was not outfitted with any mirrors.

The mirror reflects, doubles, distorts. As does disability.

Treves visited Merrick daily. Soon the doctor was able to decipher his new charge's speech. Although he initially believed Merrick to be an imbecile, Treves realized that the former sideshow freak was quite clever. Merrick spent his days reading and constructing models out of cards. He often took walks in the hospital courtyard, but only at night.

Isn't it true the monster comes out only at night?

Merrick was comfortable but lonely at the hospital. Treves arranged for a friend of his to visit, a young widow named Leila Maturin. At the meeting, Merrick was overcome with emotion. Leila was the first woman to ever shake his hand, to show him a smile. Merrick later told Treves that he wished to one day live at an institution for the blind, where he hoped to meet a woman who would not be able to see his monstrous body.

A single letter from the Elephant Man survives, written to Leila Maturin:

> *Dear Miss Maturin*
>
> *Many thanks indeed for the grouse and the book, you so kindly sent me, the grouse were splendid. I saw Mr. Treves on Sunday. He said I was to give his best respects to you.*
>
> *With much gratitude I am Yours Truly*
>
> *Joseph Merrick, London Hospital, Whitechapel*

Merrick resided at London Hospital for four years. His condition continued to deteriorate. His head would not stop growing. On April 1, 1890, Merrick was found dead in his bed. He was twenty-seven years old. Cause of death— asphyxiation. Merrick typically slept upright out of necessity, as the weight of his skull would have otherwise crushed his neck. That's how they found him. Lying down across his bed. April fool.

Dr. Treves speculated: *He often said to me that he wished he could lie down to sleep "like other people" . . . he must, with some determination, have made the experiment . . . Thus it came about that his death was due to the desire that had dominated his life—the pathetic but hopeless desire to be "like other people."*

Well-meaning people are often the most patronizing. When they know what's wrong with me, they can't resist: *Do you need help carrying that?* I shun assistance, special treatment. Pride is partly to blame. But nine times out of ten I genuinely am self-reliant, no matter how awkward I look carrying a platter to the dinner table. Constraint begets innovation.

Not that I have a choice.

Today Joseph Merrick's skeleton is housed in a glass case as part of the pathology collection at the Royal London Hospital. The Elephant Man, on display in perpetuity.

Merrick was known to quote an adapted version of Isaac Watts's poem "False Greatness":

'Tis true, my form is something odd
but blaming me, is blaming God,
Could I create myself anew
I would not fail in pleasing you.

A woman we know from the theater has a young son who was born with a rare disease. Holden is always in a wheel-chair, usually with an oxygen mask on his face. His body is swollen with fluid. He can't eat solid food. Everything is administered intravenously. He comes to see a few of our shows, parks his wheelchair in the reserved handicap spot by the front of the stage. On one occasion he draws a picture of the cast and has the usher bring it backstage for us. We all sign a poster for him. There is no cure for Holden's condition.

He dies before he turns ten. Bailey and I attend the funeral. We wait in line for the viewing. We embrace his mother. We stand in front of the tiny white casket. I stare at Holden's puffy face. I give my condolences to his mother. Every word sounds wrong, clumsy, like nothing I say matters. I excuse myself and sneak outside, where I vomit in the grass.

VII

THE VENGEANCE OF THE FLESH

I go back to school. In my American literature class, we read Raymond Carver's story "Cathedral." The unnamed narrator grows uncomfortable when an old friend of his wife's comes to visit. The man, named Robert, is blind. The narrator is at times jealous of the relationship between Robert and his wife but also mildly disgusted by the man's blindness. After the three have dinner together, everyone gets good and drunk. The wife falls asleep, leaving the narrator alone with Robert. The men smoke a joint while a television program about Gothic cathedrals plays in the background.

John Milton was forty-three years old when he became totally blind, likely the cause of glaucoma. Between 1658 and 1664 he dictated verse to his aides, and so he composed the entirety of *Paradise Lost.*

The narrator asks Robert whether he has any concept of what a cathedral looks like. When the blind man confesses that he hasn't any concrete notion, the narrator takes Robert's hand and starts drawing a cathedral so the blind man can feel the building's shape. Robert instructs the narrator to close his eyes but keep drawing. Robert asks how it looks, but the narrator decides to keep his eyes closed for a while longer. *It's really something*, he says. The narrator, who's had all of his prejudices shattered, all his preconceptions about this blind man upended, is finally able to see the truth.

We are all blind.

Of "Cathedral," Raymond Carver said, *People say it's a metaphor for some other thing, for art, for making . . . But no, I thought about the physical contact of the blind man's hand on his hand. It's all imaginary. Nothing like that ever happened to me. Well, there was an extraordinary discovery.*

Carver does not elaborate on his "extraordinary discovery."

The English musician Rick Allen garnered fame as the drummer for Def Leppard. In 1984, Allen was driving through the countryside of Sheffield when he lost control of his Corvette C4. His left arm was severed in the ensuing crash. Allen was undeterred. Instead of quitting the band, he adopted a one-armed playing style, using a customized electronic drum kit outfitted with extra foot pedals to compensate. Allen has since remarked that, if given the chance, he wouldn't change losing an arm, referring to the incident as a blessing.

Suicidal ideation is more prevalent among people with disabilities.

In George Romero's 1988 film *Monkey Shines*, Allan Mann is a promising law student who becomes a quadriplegic after a tragic traffic accident. Despondent, he attempts suicide but is saved by his best friend, the renegade scientist Geoffrey Fisher. While experimenting with a serum to boost intelligence in primates, Fisher bestows a helper monkey named Ella to the wheelchair-bound Allan. The two quickly form a close bond with unforeseen (and bloody) consequences. The drugs cause Allan and Ella to form a psychic link—symbiosis between man and monkey. Allan's personality changes. He becomes angry and aggressive, unable to repress his primal urges. Meanwhile, Ella begins killing off anyone who crosses Allan. His live-in nurse. His ex-girlfriend. His former doctor. His mother. And finally, his best friend, Fisher. A shame when good intentions come back to bite us. Literally.

Japanese researchers observed a female chimpanzee caring for its disabled offspring in the Tanzanian wilderness.

The mother managed to keep her baby alive for two years thanks to constant care, until one day in December when the researchers noted the young chimp had vanished.

Natural selection was used as justification for the Nazis' euthanasia campaign.

Charles Darwin suffered from debilitating illness for most of his adult life. He experienced a laundry list of symptoms. Heart palpitations, malaise, vertigo, dizziness, muscle spasms, vomiting, cramps, bloating, headaches, altered vision, exhaustion, dyspnea, eczema, anxiety, fainting, tachycardia, insomnia, tinnitus, depression. He tried all manner of treatments. Hydrotherapy, electric shock, laudanum. The cause remains undiagnosed.

Every year around twenty-five thousand Americans die or are permanently disabled from medical diagnostic errors.

Darwin wrote: *Age 56–57.—For 25 years extreme spasmodic daily & nightly flatulence: occasional vomiting, on two occasions prolonged during months. Vomiting preceded by shivering, hysterical crying, dying sensations or half-faint. & copious very pallid urine. Now vomiting & every paroxys of flatulence preceded by singing of ears, rocking, treading on air & vision. focus & black dots.*

I get cast in a production of *Bloody, Bloody Andrew Jackson,* a punk-rock musical about the seventh US president. One of the ensemble members is a crippled army vet named Chris. He wasn't wounded in combat but rather suffers from a degenerative nerve disease, which requires him to use a wheelchair. He asks me if I can massage his shoulders. *Muscle spasms,* he says. I feel uncomfortable because I know he's gay, but I agree because I also feel guilty knowing he's a cripple like me. I start kneading his shoulders. They don't feel too tense. He moans and tells me how good it feels. When it's our cue to enter, I push him onstage, and we start singing about the Trail of Tears. When the show closes, Chris moves to Pennsylvania, and I never see him again. One night he posts a suicide note on Facebook. His condition has worsened. First his legs, then his arms, soon his whole body will be paralyzed. He decides not to let it get any worse. A friend finds him dead in his apartment. End scene.

Twenty-seven percent of American military veterans report service-related disabilities.

The sudden onset of an illness—possibly Guillain-Barré syndrome—left Franklin D. Roosevelt permanently paralyzed from the waist down when he was thirty-nine. About a decade later, he won the presidency in a landslide victory, the only cripple ever to do so. Roosevelt was careful to conceal his disability, refusing to be seen using a wheelchair in public. During speeches, aides flanked Roosevelt on either side. He gripped the podium with both hands to support himself, gesturing with his head when needed. Only two photographs of Roosevelt in his wheelchair exist. Much of the population, including high-profile politicians, remained ignorant as to the extent of Roosevelt's handicap until the president's death in 1945.

Fellow cripple Joseph Goebbels says, *If you tell a lie big enough and keep repeating it, people will eventually come to believe it.*

Ironically, this quote is apocryphal, most likely a work of pure fiction.

If I tell myself I'm not disabled for long enough, eventually I'll come to believe it.

If I tell myself I'm not a monster for long enough, eventually I'll come to believe it.

All my assignments are late. I start a ten-page paper for my world literature class the night before it's due. I borrow liberally from scholarly articles I find online, none of which I bother to read. I crib together incoherent babble about Michael Ondaatje's *The English Patient* without attributing any sources. The professor calls me into his office. *I have some questions about your paper,* he says. *You need to be one hundred percent honest about what I'm going to ask you.* He is terse. I don't let him get any further. I look into his eyes and say, *I won't waste your time. My paper's bogus. It's a rip-off.* His face softens. He wasn't expecting me to confess so readily. He thinks for a moment and then continues: *I'll have to give you a zero on this assignment, but there's a chance you can still pass the course.* I hand him a withdrawal form. *No need,* I say. *I'm dropping out of school. I'm not well.* He signs the form and wishes me luck. *You were one of the best in the class,* he says. I close the door behind me.

Two characters in *The English Patient* are physically disabled, including the titular English patient, whose body has been burned beyond recognition, and the thief Caravaggio, whose thumbs were cut off while being tortured by Italian fascists.

Under Mussolini, the Italian government implemented sweeping social security programs, including disability insurance.

Do I qualify for disability insurance? Or am I not disabled enough?

After her failed spinal surgery, Frida completes the painting *Without Hope*. In it she lies in bed against a backdrop of volcanic rock. An enormous fleshy funnel is stuck between her lips. A mountain of viscera eases its way down the tube. Sausages, beef shanks, brains, a chicken, a turkey, a pig, a fish, and a sugar skull with "Frida" inscribed on the forehead. Bottoms up. Frida has become malnourished following the operation. Doctors prescribe a diet of pureed food to be administered every two hours. On the back of the canvas, Frida writes, *Not the least hope remains to me . . . Everything moves in time with what the belly contains.*

I sit down with my adviser, Dr. Katz. In her American lit class, she tells stories of marching with MLK, rubbing elbows with William Gass's ex-wife, pissing in an earthen pit alongside Toni Morrison at a conference in rural France. There's a framed John Waters poster in her office. She is my favorite professor. I tell her I'm dropping out again, my third time in three years. She asks me why. I explain how unmotivated I feel, how I dread coming into class, how I can't muster the energy to complete even the most trivial assignments. *I just don't care about anything,* I admit. She sees right through me: *It sounds like you're depressed.* I'm stunned. I nearly start crying. This is the first time someone has said it out loud, and as hard as I've tried to ignore reality, I know she's right.

Arbus says she's scared of getting depressed, going up and down, her mood careening, a chemical reaction causing the energy to leak from her body until even the confidence to cross a street has evaporated, leaving her terrified of things she was once eager for. She describes her condition as *quite classic.*

The French author Jean-Dominique Bauby was working as editor in chief of *Elle* when he suffered a massive stroke on December 8, 1995. When he emerged from a coma twenty days later, Bauby found himself completely paralyzed, the result of a rare condition called locked-in syndrome. Merry Christmas, Happy New Year. From then on all he could manage was to move his eyes, although his right eye had to be sewn shut because the lids stopped functioning. A speech therapist helped Bauby develop a code to communicate by blinking. With the aid of an assistant, Bauby began dictating his memoir, *The Diving Bell and the Butterfly.* Working at four-hour intervals for ten months straight, Bauby completed the book: 39,468 words, 200,000 winks.

At the book's conclusion, Bauby wonders whether the universe might contain a key to unlock his proverbial diving bell, a secret currency to buy back his freedom. He vows to keep searching.

Bauby died of pneumonia two days after the book was published.

Bailey and I have been together for almost four years when I finally meet her family. They live abroad, shuffled around by the military. First Germany, then Korea, now Hawaii. Bailey's father, Leonard, and her two younger brothers are waiting for us at Daniel K. Inouye International Airport when we step off the plane in Honolulu after a nearly twelve-hour flight. They drape leis around our necks, big purple and white orchids. Bailey was fourteen when her first brother was born, sixteen for the next. Time and distance separate them. We take H-1 and drive toward their house. I sit up front with Leonard and start trying to make a good impression. I am nervous but playing cool. Leonard is a combat veteran now operating as an interrogator for an undisclosed federal intelligence agency. I am confident he has killed people.

Despite my expectations, Leonard is cheerful. Soon we're laughing like old army buddies reunited after a long tour of duty. When we pull up to the house, Bailey's mother is just getting back from the grocery store. Darlene serves us tuna poke before we tour the house. There's a mango tree in the backyard. Small green lizards cling to the sliding glass door. Bailey and I shack up in her youngest brother's room. We share a bed shaped like a racecar. Since I can't get high, I have a vivid dream that night. I'm walking through an underground tunnel. Ahead of me, a brown bear blocks my path. *Will you be my friend?* he asks. I agree, and he lets me pass. There is a cage at the tunnel's end. I enter the cage and the bear locks me in. *Now we're friends*, he says. Then I wake to the sound of mynah birds chattering outside our window.

William Henry Johnson was the son of former slaves. As he grew, his head remained abnormally small, with a tapered skull and heavy jaw. Talent scouts from Van Emburgh's Circus spotted Johnson in Somerville, New Jersey, and offered his parents money to display the boy. P. T. Barnum later purchased the rights to exhibit Johnson, billing him as Zip the Pinhead, the "What-Is-It?" Audiences were told Zip was a missing link discovered in the jungles of Africa. Zip wore a fur suit to appear more apelike. He was kept in a cage, where he would rattle the bars and screech, much to the delight of curious crowds.

Less than human, subhuman, what the Nazis called *Untermensch*—literally, "under-man."

In the 1984 film *C.H.U.D.*, toxic waste causes members of a homeless community living in the sewers beneath New

York City to mutate. They devolve into hideous creatures with gnarled black skin and glowing yellow eyes. These C.H.U.D.—cannibalistic humanoid underground dwellers—begin preying on the city's unsuspecting populace.

More than a quarter of chronically homeless people in the United States have a disability.

I don't want to work in the café for the rest of my life so I go back to school. Fourth attempt. This time I enroll in a bunch of creative writing workshops. I submit a violent sci-fi story about a murderous pedophile. During feedback, another student declares, *Writing like this shouldn't be allowed to exist.* My professor, a magnificent poet, defends my story. She agrees the piece is disturbing but doesn't see it as an endorsement for child rape. *Literature should be challenging*, she rebuts. I know I'm onto something.

Byron says, *I am such a strange mélange of good and evil that it would be difficult to describe me.*

We sympathize with the monster for this very reason—no one is all bad.

Right?

Tsutomu might have gotten away on that hot day in July. He returns to his parked Nissan Langley sedan. Big mistake. The little girl's father calls the police after the scuffle. They are inspecting the car when Tsutomu comes creeping back. He is identified as the culprit and promptly arrested on the charge of committing indecent acts with a minor. The police soon realize that the mild-mannered young man with the funny-looking hands has done far worse.

January 12, 2013. Frederick, Maryland. My hometown. Ethan Saylor goes to see a movie with his caregiver. Ethan is twenty-six and has Down syndrome. The two catch a showing of *Zero Dark Thirty*. When the credits roll, Ethan stays behind while his caregiver fetches her car. Ethan enjoyed the movie and wants to see it again. He wanders back into the theater and returns to his seat. A manager tells Ethan he needs to buy a ticket or leave. Ethan doesn't understand; he doesn't handle money. The manager calls security. Three off-duty police officers arrive. The caregiver tries to defuse the situation, but she is barred from the theater. The officers opt to forcibly remove Ethan. All four men end up on the ground. Ethan cries out, *Mommy, it hurt!* Ethan stops breathing. His larynx is fractured. Ethan is taken to the hospital, where he is pronounced dead. The Frederick County Sheriff's Office concludes the deputies used reasonable force. A grand jury fails to indict them.

In eighth grade, I had a crush on Ethan's younger sister.

The Saylor family files an official complaint, leading to a $1.9 million settlement. In the aftermath, the State of Maryland forms the Ethan Saylor Alliance, a commission to train emergency personnel how to safely handle people with intellectual disabilities.

Between one-third and half of all people killed by police are disabled.

1950. Mexico City. Frida's health continues to decline. More surgeries. More bone grafts. More infections. More drugs. She spends a year recovering in the English Hospital. Frida tells a friend all she wants to do after leaving the hospital is *paint, paint, paint.*

Art therapy is often employed as a coping mechanism for people with disabilities. The practice has been shown to alleviate chronic pain, to improve motor and cognitive functions, and to provide a productive outlet for complex emotions.

Is that what I'm doing here?

The American artist John Callahan was twenty-one when he became a quadriplegic. He'd spent the day barhopping with a buddy, who was driving Callahan's car when they wrecked. After the accident, Callahan decided to become a cartoonist, gripping a pen between both hands to produce crude but clever one-panel gags. His macabre sense of humor and his tendency to deal in taboo subjects, most frequently disability and disease, landed him a fair share of critics, who decried Callahan's work as tasteless.

Callahan said his only compass was the reaction from people in wheelchairs or those who have hooks for hands, people like himself who were sick of being pitied and patronized. The truly detestable ones, he said, presume to speak for the freaks themselves.

In my American lit class we read Hawthorne's short story "The Birth-Mark." Aylmer is a scientist who marries the beautiful Georgiana. He finds her appearance radiant except for a small, red birthmark shaped like a hand on her left cheek. Aylmer becomes fixated on removing what he sees as Georgiana's only imperfection. He dreams of cutting the mark from his wife's cheek, the knife penetrating so deep into Georgiana's flesh that it pierces her heart. Aylmer ignores this omen, tinkering in his laboratory until he creates an elixir to rid his wife of the blemish. Georgiana realizes that even without her birthmark, Aylmer will never be satisfied. She drinks the potion anyway. As the mark fades, so too does Georgiana's life. *Do not repent that with so high and pure a feeling,* she tells her husband, *you have rejected the best the earth could offer.*

Arbus says when she sees someone, the first thing she notices is their flaws.

Matthew 7:1—*Do not judge, so that you will not be judged.*

Georges Franju's 1960 film *Eyes without a Face* revolves around Dr. Génessier, a plastic surgeon obsessed with performing a face transplant on his daughter, who was disfigured in a car crash. Christiane is kept hidden in her father's secluded mansion. He insists she wear a blank white mask to cover her scars. The mad doctor abducts young women from the surrounding Paris suburbs to use as guinea pigs for his experimental procedures. Génessier finds his powers limited, as bodies start to pile up with each failed operation. Driven insane by isolation and guilt from her father's crimes, Christiane releases a pack of German shepherds kept on the estate, the only creatures to show her affection in spite of her deformed face. The dogs attack Dr. Génessier, eviscerating his face before mauling him to death. Unfazed, Christiane walks into the forest cradling a dove in her hands.

June 17, 1816. Byron vacations at the Villa Diodati near Lake Geneva, accompanied by Percy Blythe Shelley and Mary Wollstonecraft Godwin (Percy's eighteen-year-old mistress who will soon become his wife). Confined to the house because of incessant rain, Byron proposes a contest. The three will each write a ghost story. Byron pens an unfinished draft of a vampire tale called "A Fragment." Shelley attempts to write something based on his childhood but soon gives up. Mary, the least experienced writer of the trio, also struggles to conceive an idea. She's been having trouble sleeping, haunted by dreams of her daughter, who was born premature and died the previous year. During a night of insomnia, Mary has a vision: *I saw the pale student of unhallowed arts kneeling beside the thing he had put together. I saw the hideous phantasm of a man stretched out, and then, on the working of some powerful engine, show signs of life, and stir with an uneasy, half vital motion. Frightful must it be; for supremely frightful would be the effect of any human endeavour to mock the stupendous mechanism of the Creator of the world.*

I write an adaptation of Mary Shelley's *Frankenstein* for the stage. It is a fractured, fragmented rendition of the classic story told with kinetic choreography and nightmare logic. I play Dr. Victor Frankenstein. To my surprise, the production is well received. Audience members corner me after a performance to gush about how thought-provoking they found the piece. Funny, all this attention for one lousy cripple.

The iconic Frankenstein's monster, this modern Prometheus, has been portrayed by everyone from Boris Karloff to Benedict Cumberbatch. The creature tells his maker, *I was benevolent; my soul glowed with love and humanity: but am I not alone, miserably alone? You, my creator, abhor me; what hope can I gather from your fellow-creatures, who owe me nothing? they spurn and hate me.*

Is the monster evil from inception? Or might he not have turned murderous if he'd been shown the slightest affection?

With Tsutomu in custody, police conduct a search of the young man's apartment, where they find nearly six thousand videotapes—anime, slasher flicks, child pornography. Among his collection are recordings and photographs of the victims. Tsutomu soon confesses. He blames his deformed hands for his antisocial behavior and alienation. Tsutomu tells police, *If I tried to talk to my parents about my problems, they'd just brush me off. I even thought about suicide.*

August 24, 1941. Facing pressure from prominent religious leaders, Hitler gives the order to suspend the T4 program. But the killings are far from over. A second phase takes shape, what became known as "wild euthanasia." Doctors are permitted to act on their own accord. As long as they keep it quiet, medical officials decide who will live and who will die. For the next several years, the doctors remain busy.

A Monster Science Created—But Could Not Destroy!

Bailey and I take a trip to Philadelphia. We eat salmon curry at the Reading Terminal Market. I spend a few hours in a used bookstore while Bailey shops for clothes. We tour the Mütter Museum, home to more than twenty thousand anatomical anomalies. There's a wall of 139 skulls, little plaques bearing names and causes of death. Slides of Einstein's brain tissue. A plaster cast of the famed conjoined twins Chang and Eng Bunker. A two-headed fetus preserved in formaldehyde. A wax replica of a Frenchwoman called Widow Sunday from whose forehead sprouted an eight-inch horn. I imagine one day my severed arms might be displayed here in a glass case, worth the price of admission alone.

The cost of a ticket to see the Elephant Man was twopence.

During his final years, Goya withdrew from public life. He moved to an old farmhouse on the edge of Madrid known as La Quinta del Sordo—The Country House of the Deaf Man. Solitude for the master but little peace. Goya dreaded old age. Long-standing anxieties of going mad persisted. At age seventy-five he produced what would become some of his most famous work, the Black Paintings, eschewing canvas for the plaster walls of his home. Imagine sitting down for a meal in the dining room only to be confronted with *Saturn Devouring His Son*, the wild-haired Titan's haunted stare surveying your plate.

And what of you? Would you destroy your own child? Perhaps before he was born? If you knew he would come out wrong?

The Japanese writer Kenzaburō Ōe's son Hikari was born mentally disabled, the result of a brain hernia. For more than a month after the birth, Ōe debated whether to proceed with a surgery that would save Hikari's life or to simply let the boy die. This experience is mirrored in Ōe's

1964 novel *A Personal Matter*. The narrator, simply called Bird, abandons his wife at the hospital to go on a drinking binge and shack up with his mistress, secretly hoping the "monster baby" will not survive. He pushes a pediatrician to feed the baby sugar water instead of milk to speed up the process. To his surprise, the doctors expect the baby will survive if given surgery, although they warn Bird that his son will never be normal. Frantic, Bird brings the baby to a back-alley abortionist and pays to have him euthanized. In the final four pages, Bird calls off the plan and returns his baby to the hospital for surgery. The real-life Hikari grew up to become a respected composer of classical music whose first album sold more than any of his father's books.

The first painting Frida finishes after her back surgery is *Self-Portrait with the Portrait of Doctor Farill*, a gift for the man who performed the operation, much like Goya's *Self-Portrait with Dr. Arrieta* from 131 years prior. Frida stares out coyly, sitting in a wheelchair, a heart-shaped palette in her hands. There is a painting within the painting, a mise en abyme of Dr. Farill, whose unibrow mirrors Frida's. His compassionate gaze points toward Frida, but their eyes do not meet. The doctor has saved his patient's life, but he can never truly know her suffering.

The same way you look at a cripple. Your view is forever unfinished, incomplete.

I earn a bachelor's degree in 2015. I'm twenty-five years old. I quit my job at the café and start tutoring part-time at a local community college. The wages are a fraction of what I made serving coffee and bagels. I start applying for master's programs, thinking I can be a professor someday. I pay the fees, fill out the forms, secure letters of recommendation. After a few months, I receive a series of curt rejection letters. All my attempts have failed. My bank account dwindles, credit card debt swells.

More than a quarter of households in the United States with at least one disabled family member have medical debt.

The traditionally conservative view that Social Security benefits are an entitlement and therefore subject to budgetary cuts.

The traditionally conservative view that abortion is wrong because all life is precious.

The hard reality of the fiscal burden that caring for a disabled family member entails.

Paradox—a woman should be forced to carry a crippled baby to term, but she shouldn't be provided the slightest bit of support to give that same child a decent quality of life.

Greg Abbott, the firebrand conservative governor of Texas, was paralyzed from the waist down when he was twenty-six. A falling branch from an oak tree struck Abbott as he was out jogging after a rainstorm. Abbott sued the landowner, resulting in an insurance settlement totaling $8 million.

How's that for a handout?

One year before winning the 2016 presidential election, Donald Trump mocks disabled journalist Serge Kovaleski at a campaign rally. He makes an exaggerated, exasperated expression while flailing his arms: *Uhh! I don't know what I said! Uhhh! I don't remember!* Kovaleski has arthrogryposis, a congenital condition that contracts the body's joints, sometimes causing limp wrists. Despite having won a Pulitzer, Kovaleski will forever be remembered as the disabled guy who Trump made fun of. Such is the power of a bully.

I can still hear them snickering: *Matt's got retard arms!*

March 30, 1990. Four months before I'm born, Tsuto-mu's trial begins. The proceedings will last for seven years. Tsutomu often rambles nonsensically in court. He blames his crimes on an alter ego called "Rat Man," who Tsutomu claims forced him to kill. Three teams of court-appointed psychiatrists evaluate Tsutomu. They all draw different conclusions. In the end, the court finds Tsutomu fully capable of taking responsibility for his actions. He describes the murders as *an act of benevolence.*

Bailey and I are both cast in an adaptation of *Oedipus Rex.* The mythic hero's name comes from the Greek word *Oidípous,* meaning "swollen foot." Oedipus's feet are delib-erately maimed at birth, but that doesn't stop him from fulfilling the Oracle's prophecy and killing his father, King Laius, at a crossroads. Nor does it prevent him from solv-ing the Sphinx's riddle, ascending the throne of Thebes, marrying his mother, and siring four children with her, ultimately dooming Jocasta to suicide when the truth is revealed. The guilt-ridden Oedipus gouges out his eyes, as if being lame weren't enough of a handicap. Quite the résumé for a crippled motherfucker.

Hob Broun describes writing as groping blind, clicking together ideas with no idea how everything will add up.

Before being paralyzed, Broun's work was fueled by guilt. Unable to move, writing became his reason to live.

Mom moves to Ken's place in southern Maryland near the Patuxent River. Bailey and I move into Mom's old house, the one I grew up in. I start cleaning out the basement. The slate foundation is so decrepit and porous that water seeps through whenever there is rain. Yellow mold populates the wooden ceiling beams. I take a bleach-soaked sponge across the splinters and rusty nails, spray vinegar to ward off the spores. I know they will return. I find a box full of my papers from grade school that Mom saved. She never throws anything away. I sort the musty pages, preserve a few, my first short stories. There is a paper plate with a tracing of my hand transformed into a Thanksgiving turkey. I study a worksheet prompt: *I felt lonely when* . . . My six-year-old scratch tells me I was sad when other kids teased me, but I expressed optimism for the future. I can't look anymore. The garbage men make off with the rotten scraps in the morning.

The performance artist Stelarc bases most of his pieces around a central thesis—the human body is obsolete. In much of his work, Stelarc incorporates cybernetic prosthesis into his own flesh. A robotic third arm. A pneumatic exoskeleton with spiderlike legs. A cell-cultivated ear surgically attached to his left forearm.

When zombies rip off the leg of go-go dancer Cherry Darling in the film *Planet Terror*, she replaces the missing limb with an assault rifle.

When the white whale Moby Dick bites off Ahab's leg, the mad captain replaces the lost appendage with a whalebone.

Let us count the ways our corporeal vessels might be modified.

Sometimes for the better. More often, not.

A friend tips me off to a gig at a military hospital near DC. The army brings in actors to play patients for training students. Some weeks I'm a person with schizophrenia plotting to murder his boss. Other times I'm a navy corpsman delirious with fever after contracting malaria while digging wells in Laos. Occasionally I'm a gunshot victim in a mass shooting, or I've had my arm blown off in a terrorist attack. I get covered in fake blood, with rubber intestines poking out of my shirt, and I writhe screaming in imagined agony on the ground as the emergency responder trainees pretend to administer first aid and load me onto a stretcher. The top brass in their crisp white uniforms tell us we're serving our country. One day I'm sitting in the staged exam room wearing a hospital gown and explaining my symptoms to a nursing student. Cough, fatigue, poor concentration. The nurse asks me to hold out my arm. He twists my hand and I cry out in pain. *Sorry! Just checking your pulse.* I stay in character. I tell him about my condition. I try to steer the conversation back on script: *That's not why I came to see you today.* He studies my forearm: *Wild. I read about this. Never seen it in real life before.* But it's not real life. It's a carefully controlled scenario. I'm an actor playing a part. Still, my body remains indifferent. The finest performance I can muster will never be enough. My hands will not obey.

In Shakespeare's *Titus Andronicus*, the titular general's daughter Lavinia is abducted during a royal hunt. After raping Lavinia, her captors cut off the girl's hands and tongue to keep her from revealing their identities. Later, Lavinia uses a stick clenched between her teeth to spell out the rapists' names in the dirt. But not before Titus is tricked into cutting off his own left hand.

August 1953. In an effort to stop the spread of gangrene, doctors amputate Frida's right leg at the knee. Before the surgery, Frida writes in her diary that she is worried but expects a sense of liberation will follow. Frida is outfitted with a prosthetic limb. She jokes with friends about her peg leg. She learns to dance the jarabe tapatío on the wooden limb, sporting red leather boots embroidered with gold and decorated with little bells. The pain persists. The doctors cannot remove her battered spine. Frida drinks two liters of cognac every day. She injects large doses of the painkiller Demerol. Her body is covered in scabs. She sinks into a deep depression. Six months after the operation, Frida writes in her diary that she wants to kill herself. For nearly a year she paints nothing.

When the monster transforms and rampages, he often awakes the next morning with no memory of the carnage left behind.

There are so many nights I do not remember.

Dr. Jekyll says, *I sometimes think if we knew all, we should be more glad to get away.*

Bailey's parents and brothers move back to Maryland. To celebrate their homecoming, they organize a family trip to Disney World. We fly to Orlando and check into the resort. A bungalow on stilts surrounded by jungle foliage meticulously constructed to appear rustic and natural. Small brown lizards skitter across the path as we haul our suitcases up the stairs. Each day we hit a different park. I maintain a steady buzz exploring Epcot. Twenty-dollar margarita in Mexico. Grand Marnier slushie in France. Strong brown beer in England. I ride roller coasters with Bailey's younger brothers and try not to puke. I float in countless crystal-clear chlorinated pools watching families in matching T-shirts squabble over ticket prices. A man in a Goofy suit hugs me, and I do not want to let go.

A wide range of disabilities present themselves in the Disney canon. The seven dwarfs. The Hunchback of Notre Dame. Nemo and his withered flipper. Captain Hook.

To pass the time, I read Stanley Elkin's *The Magic Kingdom*. In the novel, a group of terminally ill British children are taken to Disney World as a consolation prize, a dream vacation for kids who will never get to grow up. The seven lucky (?) kiddos offer a cornucopia of grotesqueries— cystic fibrosis, congenital heart disease, ovarian cancer, premature aging, Gaucher disease, leukemia, bone cancer. Watching the endless parade of tourists, a nurse consoles the dying children, pointing out the aging, sagging, corrupted flesh. The dying children, explains the nurse, are not missing out on anything.

Elkin himself suffered from multiple sclerosis for much of
his life. He once said the diagnosis didn't affect his writing
stylistically but did give him more opportunity to concen-
trate, as he was stuck in a wheelchair most of the time.

The nurse continues watching the crowd, saying it breaks
her heart, the omnipresent imperfection, the unavoidable
wear and tear, the plethora of bodies endlessly straying
from their true form.

In 2017 I am twenty-seven, working odd jobs, frequently
broke. I still tutor at the community college a few days
every week. Althea is a student who often comes to see
me. She can hear but cannot speak. I suspect she has an
intellectual disability, but the law bars me from inquiring.
We work on an essay about the civil rights movement. She
writes about being Black and how people have mistreated
her. I want to help Althea pass her freshman comp class.
She struggles with elaborating her ideas. I make an outline for her, give her a stack of writing guides. There are
long periods when her attention drifts as she compulsively
rubs a pencil eraser against her notebook and then eats the
rubber shavings. I try to discourage the habit. Weeks pass.
Progress is slow. Other assignments are due, but Althea
still hasn't finished the first. At the end of the semester,
her mother comes into the library and berates the staff.

Althea flunked the class. Her mother blames us. Campus security hustles her out. I never see Althea again.

The cripple is an inconvenience. He requires accommodations. He disrupts your routine.

The monster is a nightmare. He manifests your deepest fears. He needs your blood.

Brandon, another regular, comes into the college library for tutoring again, carting his shabby backpack on wheels. I'm on duty, and Brandon needs help with a paper. We sit together at a computer beneath the dusty air vent and its frigid air. I never learn exactly how old Brandon is. Maybe eighteen or nineteen. I never learn exactly what is wrong with him. His pockmarked face is pinched in like he's constantly sucking a lemon. A stream of spittle dribbles from his fish-thin lips. His black doll eyes are shiny and nervous. He has a scrawny, stooped stick frame, his clothes always too big, ghost-billowing around his snappable body. His dark hair is matted, unwashed, greasy. He speaks only in monosyllables: *Yes. No. Um.* I never hear him string together a full sentence. He pulls up his assignment on the screen. I smile. *Ready to begin, Brandon?* Silence. *I'll read this out loud. We'll talk about what you've written. We'll get it cleaned up, OK?* Silence. I recite his work. Incomprehensible babble. *What are you trying to say here?* Silence. I watch the saliva drip from his chicken-skinned chin. *What if we wrote it like this?* I type a fresh line. *Is this what you mean?* Silence. I give him some advice, some recommendations, some prompts. I write a few more examples. *Our time is up, Brandon. I'll let you work on your own for now. Does what I wrote make sense?* His slack jaw moves at last. *Yes.* I try not to think it, but I do. *This poor fuck ought to be put out of his misery.*

And just like that, I'm thinking like a Nazi.

I sit down with Jackie for tutoring. She has severe cerebral palsy and uses a walker. She cannot speak. She communicates by typing notes on an iPad. Her lips are always pursed, tongue jutting out. She is writing an essay about the American dream. Her work is eloquent, clear-sighted, deep. She wants me to read for grammatical errors. I don't find many. Jackie's dream is to earn her associate degree and transfer to a four-year college. She wants to pursue social work, to help people. She doesn't need my help. Jackie is the one teaching me.

Of her subjects, Diane Arbus says they tend to like her. She dotes on the people she photographs. *Terrific!* she tells a disfigured woman as the shutter clicks. Yes, such a face is undeniably amazing, but Arbus would never want to look like that, want her children to look like that, want to kiss a face so twisted.

I get cast in a production of Deborah Zoe Laufer's *End Days*. In the play, one of the characters hallucinates that she's being visited by the astrophysicist Stephen Hawking. All of Hawking's dialogue is prerecorded in his trademark computerized voice. The scenes never fail to garner huge laughs from the audience.

Stephen Hawking was diagnosed with motor neuron disease when he was twenty-one, during his final year studying at Oxford. Doctors estimated he would live another two years at best. Although he survived much longer, the disease gradually robbed Hawking of most of his basic faculties over the course of several decades. By the end, Hawking was confined to a wheelchair, famously communicating through an electronic speech-generating device that he controlled by twitching a muscle in his cheek.

What's the difference between Stephen Hawking and the computer he's hooked up to?

When an interviewer asked how he wished to be remembered, Hawking replied: first, as a scientist, second, as a writer; and above all as a normal human being with dreams, desires, and ambitions like anyone else.

The computer runs.

Hawking met his first wife, Jane, only a year before his diagnosis. Jane stood by her ailing husband for thirty years, until the good doctor dumped her for his nurse, Elaine Mason. This new union was not without its own strife. Allegations surfaced that Elaine was abusive. At one point she left Hawking outside until he had sunstroke. Unexplained cuts and bruises appeared on Hawking's helpless body. He refused to press charges, even after the couple quietly divorced.

I'm accepted into a master's program at a state school just outside Baltimore. I make the hour-long drive to campus three nights a week. On the recommendation of my adviser, I enroll in a creative nonfiction course. After a few weeks of workshops, I suspect the professor is brilliant. Reading her book confirms this. We're assigned contemporary memoirs to study and critique. We write essays of our own and pick them apart in the hopes of improving our work. We are instructed to point out what we notice about one another's writing rather than what we like or dislike. *Write about what makes you uncomfortable,* she tells us. I know immediately which subject to interrogate.

Katherine Dunn's novel *Geek Love* follows the saga of the Binewskis, a family of traveling carnies. To save their failing business, Al and Crystal decide to use drugs and toxic waste as a means of breeding mutated children for a freak show. Siamese twins. A hunchbacked dwarf. A tele- kinetic. Their son Arty the Aqua Boy, who has flippers for hands and feet, develops a sadomasochistic cult in which members must amputate their own limbs. The worse the deformity, Arty logics, the greater the sanctity.

No sense in being resentful. No sense in being grateful, either. Acceptance is all I ask.

Is this why I'm drawn to horror films? Within the mon- ster, do I recognize myself?

I *have* a disability.

I *am* disabled.

Which is it?

Something I possess.

Something deeper.

You wouldn't say, *I have a monstrosity.*

No.

You would say, *I am a monster.*

I've always said *my condition* rather than *my disability.* A condition is vague, an ambiguous state of being. A condition could be anything. A disability is finite, concrete, definitive. A disability puts you into a rigid category. All cripples have conditions, but not everyone with a condition can be labeled "a cripple."

What of the monster? What is his condition? Evil, frightening, grotesque. Alone, miserable, abject. His monstrosity is both handicap and superpower. Either way, he is cursed.

After seven years together, Bailey says, *You'll never marry me.* I decide to prove her wrong. I buy a ring from a Canadian jeweler. Stamped sterling silver band. Raw white diamond. I suggest a trip to New York. I haven't visited the city since I moved back home. We take the train. Bright spring day. Warm enough to walk around in a T-shirt. We unload our baggage at the one-bedroom apartment we've rented. Spicy lamb noodles for lunch. *Let's go to the High Line*, I say, pulling Bailey along Eleventh Avenue, noodles churning my guts. Along the High Line's winding path, I spot a small balcony overlooking the Hudson. There's another couple there taking a photo. We wait our turn. I look at Bailey and ask, *What should we do tonight?* She says, *I don't know. What do you think?* Hand in my pocket, fingers around the little black box: *Depends how you answer this question.* I'm down on my knee holding the ring. I can hear passersby chittering with delight. I ask Bailey to marry me, and she's crying and nodding her head, and she can barely get the word out, but she does. She says yes, and I put the ring on her finger, and the small crowd gathered to watch cheers and applauds. A short, stout abuela comes running over: *This is a special moment. I took your picture.* She asks for my phone number, texts me the candid shot. A Buddhist monk materializes in front of me and slips a brown-beaded bracelet onto my wrist. He says, *Happiness*, and I thank him, but when I try to walk away he says, *Happiness!* He sounds angry, and I realize he wants money for the bracelet. I pull out a five, but he wants twenty. I say, *This is all I have*, and the disgruntled monk takes my last five dollars and disappears into the crowd.

In Larry Cohen's 1974 film *It's Alive*, Frank and Lenore Davis are expecting their second child. Instead of a healthy baby boy, Lenore delivers a deformed monster with razor-sharp claws and fangs. The newborn mutant escapes and goes on a rampage, killing the couple's first son by biting out his throat. Frank manages to corner the creature in the sewers but cannot bring himself to kill it. With tears in his eyes, he lowers his rifle and scoops the whimpering baby in his arms: *Shhh . . . It's gonna be all right . . . It's gonna be all right.*

In the end we think the monster is dead. Until he opens his eyes and lunges. Fake out.

In 1994, Tsutomu's father commits suicide by jumping into a river. He cannot reconcile the pain his son has caused. Tsutomu responds, *I feel refreshed.*

The protagonists of Doris Lessing's 1988 novel *The Fifth Child* are wealthy couple David and Harriett Lovatt. They live a life of comfort and ease in the English countryside, raising four beautiful, bourgeois children. The arrival of their fifth child upends their idyllic existence. Something isn't right with Ben. His body is muscular, yellowish, long. His head is misshapen. His forehead slopes. His skin is sallow, lumpish. Worst of all, he's highly aggressive. When Harriett tries to breastfeed Ben, he bites her nipples until they're black. He grows stronger, more sadistic. Dead pets start turning up around the neighborhood. He sprains his older brother's arm seemingly for the fun of it. Desperate for the nightmare to end, Harriett has Ben institutionalized. But when she goes to visit the boy and finds him straitjacketed among what she describes as *rows of freaks*, Harriett immediately decides to bring Ben home, knowing it will destroy her family.

Kristeva says the apex of abjection occurs when death interferes with the forces meant to save us—youth or science—like when we walk through the halls of Auschwitz and see a pile of children's shoes.

I wish you could know what it's like, but you never will.

I wish I could know what it's like, but I never will.

There are only 350 cases of congenital radioulnar synostosis documented in medical journals. The global population is nearly eight billion.

What are the odds?

You do the math.

Congenital radioulnar synostosis is due to abnormal fetal development of the forearm bones. The underlying cause is unknown. Chromosomes gone awry. Genetic mutations. Unlucky inheritance. Act of God.

Preordained fate or random chance?

Most monsters have a backstory, a reason for their hideous nature, a motivation for their wicked ways. At least they know.

Wish I could say the same.

Today, radioulnar synostosis can be corrected with surgery if performed in early childhood.

I'm thirty years too late.

Would I change it if I could? Take part in some miracle procedure and let my hands be fixed?

No.

This is who I am, who I have always been.

I am content to be a cripple.

What of my mistakes? Given the chance, would I undo them? Take back the pain I've caused?

Yes.

Since revising the past is impossible, all I can do is admit to my errors, own every sin, and work to never repeat them, to do better. My hands are irreparable. My behavior is not.

Deformity does not define the monster. His actions do.

My hands have never made me feel like a monster. My words, deeds. My excuses, lies. My callousness, shallowness. My contempt, spite. My immaturity, flippancy. My lust, aggression. This is what makes me a monster.

My hands have embarrassed me, frustrated me. They turn me into a little boy again, awkward, insecure. I don't want to be a joke. I don't want pity. I don't want to explain what's wrong with me. I don't want to hide.

I want to put my arms around you, my hands resting flat against your back, fingers notched along your spine. I want to pull you in close and cup my hands behind your shoulders. I want to palm the back of your head.

But I cannot. I never will.

I put my arms around you, thumbs brushing your back, knuckles dragging across ribs. I pull you close and tuck my hands in your armpits. I rub the back of your head with the top of my hand.

Am I good enough for you?

VIII

BIGGER THAN LIFE

May 1, 1945. Berlin. Joseph Goebbels is depressed. The Führer is dead. The Soviets are rapidly advancing. The Reichland is in ruins. Goebbels instructs an SS dentist to inject his six children with morphine. When they're unconscious, cyanide capsules are crushed in their mouths. Goebbels escorts his wife, Magda, to the Chancellery gardens, where the couple shoot themselves. Forty-seven and forty-three years old, respectively. Their bodies are doused in petrol and set alight. Berlin falls. The Soviets identify the charred corpses, which are kept at a storage facility for twenty-five years, until the remains are formally ordered to be destroyed—burned, crushed, and scattered into the river Ehle.

May 19, 1945. Altaussee. Philipp Bouhler, the SS official who oversaw the Aktion T4 program, has been arrested by American troops at Schloss Fischhorn. While being held at an internment camp, Bouhler swallows cyanide. Forty-five years old. The blood of nearly three hundred thousand cripples on his hands.

May 29, 1945. Bavaria. Richard Jenne is a disabled patient at the children's ward of Kaufbeuren-Irsee state hospital. He is euthanized by lethal injection. Four years old. American troops have occupied the town for more than three weeks.

I need you to look at the last photograph taken of Richard.

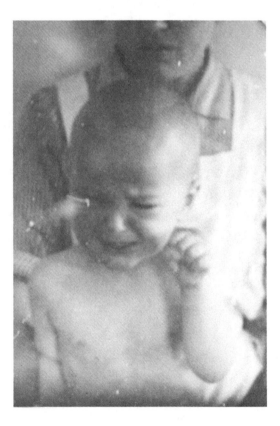

June 2, 1948. Landsberg Prison. Karl Brandt, co-head of the Aktion T4 program, has been charged and convicted of crimes against humanity at the Nuremberg trials. He is sentenced to death. Forty-four years old. On the gallows, Brandt says, *It is no shame to stand upon the scaffold. This is nothing but political revenge. I have served my Fatherland as others before me.* When he refuses to end his speech, a hood is placed over his head. He is still talking when the rope goes taut.

July 13, 1954. Mexico City. Frida Kahlo is still stuck at La Casa Azul. She sketches a black angel in her diary. She writes, *I hope the exit is joyful—and I hope never to return.* She's run a high fever all night. Excruciating pain. A nurse finds Frida's body in her bed. Forty-seven years old. The official cause of death is listed as pulmonary embolism. Some suspect Frida has in fact committed suicide. An inventory of her medication reveals Frida swallowed eleven painkillers the night before she died. Frida is cremated. To this day she remains at La Casa Azul, her ashes displayed in a toad-shaped urn.

October 6, 1962. His reputation ruined after *Freaks*, Tod Browning directs only four other films before abandoning Hollywood altogether. He retreats from the public eye after his wife, Alice, dies of pneumonia. Browning spends the next two decades holed up in Malibu. A recluse. A drunk. Develops cancer of the larynx. An operation leaves him mute. The cancer won't quit. He dies alone. Eighty-two years old. Friends find his body in the bathroom.

July 26, 1971. New York City. Diane Arbus is in her apartment at Westbeth Artists Community. Unit A, floor 9, number 945. She places her appointment book on the stairs leading to the bathroom. In her diary she writes, *Last Supper*. She swallows barbiturates and runs a bath. Lying in the tub, she slashes her wrists. Forty-eight years old. Her body is discovered two days later.

August 14, 1972. Eddie Carmel, the "Jewish Giant," has a heart attack. He is rushed to Montefiore Hospital in the Bronx, where he dies. Thirty-six years old. His body is buried in a custom-built coffin.

December 16, 1987. Portland, Oregon. Hob Broun is home working on his third novel. His respirator malfunctions. Air stops pumping. Hob Broun asphyxiates. Thirty-seven years old. He leaves his novel unfinished.

June 17, 2008. Tokyo Detention House. Minister of Justice Kunio Hatoyama signs Tsutomu Miyazaki's death warrant. Tsutomu has never apologized, never expressed remorse. He is hanged. Forty-five years old. His final words: *I'm going to get you, Batman! I swear! If it's the last thing I do!*

October 3, 2013. San Francisco. Lisa Bufano posts two photos to Facebook. A picture of her face, exhausted. A picture of a room, empty. She takes her own life. Forty years old. She does not leave a note. The means are not made public.

The year is 2020. Eight months after the wedding we're in lockdown. People like to ask, *Aren't you glad you got married last year?* I finish grad school, remotely, but I still can't land a job. We march in a local Black Lives Matter protest during a torrential downpour. We celebrate our first anniversary at home. Some takeout, a few drinks. The same week my stepfather, Ken, has a stroke. Mom rushes him to the hospital. She has to wait in the parking lot. Ken almost dies. He's transferred to a hospital in DC. Stays in the stroke ward for a month. Mom drives a two-hour round trip to see him every day. When he's discharged, Ken is not the same. He can barely walk, talk. His mind is not right. He's forced to retire early, falls into a depression, lashes out at the people trying to help him. We're told this is all normal. Mom takes care of him. Feeds him, bathes him, drives him to countless doctor appointments.

Not once do I hear her complain. She tells me, *I love him. This is what I was meant to do.*

If the monster acknowledges the pain he has caused and renounces his wicked ways, would you give him another chance? Does the beast deserve mercy? Do I?

My first novel is published around the same time Trump loses his reelection campaign. We celebrate at home. Some takeout, a few drinks. I've been trying to cut back. I keep pecking away at the new manuscript—this one. People keep dying. Millions. Life goes on. Just before Christmas, Bailey buys a pregnancy test. Two pink lines appear on the innocuous white stick.

Two lines. Two hands.

Nine months later. August 19, 2021. 3:52 A.M. At the hospital a midwife pulls my boy from between Bailey's legs after three hours of pushing. The baby comes out wet and bloody and screaming. Bailey holds him to her breast. We laugh and cry as the nurses cheer. They whisk the baby away for a bevy of tests. There's nothing wrong. A perfectly healthy baby boy. Not a monster. Might he become one? A possibility. Could a monster come take him away? A chance. My boy is pure potential.

The stocky nurse brings him back to me, puts the baby in my arms. He is just under eight pounds. I look at his scrunched face, his curious eyes. I see myself reflected in his gray irises.

Infinity awaits us.

Hello, Umberto.

I hold him.

ACKNOWLEDGMENTS

I would like to express my gratitude to the following people who were instrumental to the composition of this book.

Thank you, Jeannie Vanasco, for nurturing this project from its inception, offering feedback and guidance inside and outside the classroom. I would never have dreamed of writing creative nonfiction without your mentorship.

Thank you, Marisa Emily Siegel, for believing in this project and finding a home for the book. Your editorial insight and encouragement have been invaluable.

Thank you, Courtney Smotherman, for helping me navigate the complexities of copyright law in referencing dozens of sources throughout this book.

Thank you, Anne Gendler, Katherine Faydash, and Ariana Tyler, for the incisive edits and suggestions.

Thank you, Joann Foltz, my mother, for your strength, creativity, and love. I owe you everything.

Thank you, Bailey Sterling-Lee, my wife, for making me want to be a better person. I love you.

Thank you, Umberto, my son, for bringing me joy I never thought possible. You are my greatest inspiration.

Finally, I would like to honor the countless cripples who have come before me, and countless others who will follow, for resisting injustice, ignorance, hatred, and violence— far too often at the expense of their lives. Never forget, to maintain hope for a better world in the face of insurmountable opposition is a radical act. Fight on.

NOTES

I. The Creature Walks among Us

5 *Let the shameful wall of exclusion finally come tumbling down.* George H. W. Bush, "Remarks of President George H. W. Bush at the Signing of the Americans with Disabilities Act," Civil Rights Division, US Department of Justice, July 26, 1990. https://archive.ada.gov/ghw_bush_ada_rcmarks .html. The roots of the Americans with Disabilities Act (ADA) can be traced to the Reagan administration, when George H. W. Bush was vice president and reviewed the initial conceptual report. Bush was intimately familiar with disability and illness, as his son, Neil, was born with learning disabilities, and his daughter, Robin, died of leukemia when she was three years old.

6 *We didn't lie to you, folks. Freaks,* directed by Tod Browning (1932; Beverly Hills, CA: Metro-Goldwyn-Mayer, 2005), DVD. Dialogue from the opening scene of the film; the carnival barker is played by Murray Kinnell.

7 **The philosopher Julia Kristeva describes abjection . . .** Julia Kristeva, *Powers of Horror: An Essay on Abjection,* trans. Leon S. Roudiez (New York: Columbia University Press, 1984). Kristeva has written extensively on disability, a subject in which she was fatefully enmeshed after her son, David, was born with a sensorimotor disorder that affects his cognitive ability.

8 ***Let there be a law that no deformed child shall live.*** Aristotle, *Politics*, trans. Benjamin Jowett (Kitchener: Batoche Books, 1999), 178. Aristotle echoes Plato, who argued parents should dispose of children born deficient. For Aristotle, a code of eugenics was part of his envisioned ideal city.

10 ***Cripples, take heart, and may your affairs prosper.*** Donna McDonald, "Visual Narratives: Contemplating the Storied Images of Disability and Disablement," in *The Routledge Handbook of Disability Arts, Culture, and Media*, ed. Bree Hadley and Donna McDonald (Oxfordshire: Routledge, 2018), 41. The original Flemish inscription is in a fragmentary state. This translation/reconstruction comes from the Louvre.

12 **. . . a young man spat on one of Arbus's prints.** Tessa DeCarlo, "A Fresh Look at Diane Arbus," *Smithsonian Magazine*, May 2004, https://www.smithsonianmag.com/arts-culture/a-fresh-look-at-diane-arbus-99861134. The target of the viewer's outrage (and saliva) was *A Young Man in Curlers at Home on West 20th Street, NYC*, which depicts a male subject in drag.

12 ***Do you want to be made well?*** John 5:6-8. All biblical citations are from the online World English Bible.

13 **Numerous religious organizations opposed the Americans with Disabilities Act . . .** Kim A. Lawton, "Churches 'Live with' Disabilities Act," *Christianity Today* 34, no. 14 (October 8, 1990): 71. Beyond fiscal concerns, certain factions of ultra-conservative evangelicals also balked at the notion that the ADA would protect people with HIV.

14 **In the Bible, visual impairment is considered among the lowest degradations.** The correlation between sin, darkness, and blindness is evident in both the Old and New Testament. Sinners are struck blind for their transgressions, as was the case with the wicked men of Sodom (Genesis 19:11) and the magician Elymas, who obstructed the work of Paul (Acts 13:4–12). Christ, meanwhile, attributes blindness to lack of faith, drawing a parallel between visual impairment and spiritual blindness (Mark 10:52).

15 **A Punnett square shows the odds: 50-50.** Harold Chen, "Congenital Radioulnar Synostosis," in *Atlas of Genetic Diagnosis and Counseling* (New York: Springer, 2017), 627–33. Although the occurrence of radioulnar synostosis can be random, patterns of familial autosomal dominant inheritance have been reported in several case studies. Across the literature, there is some debate on the frequency of genetic inheritance, with Boston Children's Hospital noting that around one in five, or 20 percent, of its patients treated for radioulnar synostosis have a family member with the same condition.

18 *Offend one and you offend them all.* Browning, *Freaks*.

21 **During the eugenics movement of the early twentieth century** . . . Stafan Kuhl, *The Nazi Connection: Eugenics, American Racism, and German National Socialism* (Oxford: Oxford University Press, 2002), 17. In 1907, Indiana enacted the first law allowing for the sterilization of mentally disabled people. A further thirty states followed, and the last compulsory sterilization law in the United States was not repealed until 1974.

II. The Disembodied

25   *One of us, one of us. Gooble gobble, gooble gobble.* Browning, *Freaks.*

26   **The dwarfs were deported to their home countries.** Janet Ravenscroft, "Dwarfs—and a Loca—as Ladies' Maids at the Spanish Habsburg Courts," in *The Politics of Female Households: Ladies-in-Waiting across Early Modern Europe*, ed. Nadine Akkerman and Birgit Houben (Leiden: Brill, 2014), 172. Maria Bárbola, also known as Maribárbola Asquín, was part of the royal household for almost fifty years and earned the title of "Enana de la Reina"—the queen's dwarf—before her deportation.

27   *Anyone who considers this entertainment should be placed in the pathological ward in some hospital.* Harrison's Reports, July 16, 1932, 114. In the wake of such negative reviews, MGM issued a press release to counter accusations that the studio had exploited the disabled cast: "What about abnormal people? They have their lives, too!"

27   *There is no excuse for this picture.* John C. Moffitt, *Kansas City (MO) Star*, quoted in David J. Skal and Elias Savada, *Dark Carnival: The Secret World of Tod Browning* (New York: Anchor Books, 1995), 178. A handful of contemporary critics reviewed *Freaks* in a (somewhat) favorable light, notably the *New York Times* and *The New Yorker*, and the film's reputation steadily improved from the 1960s onward. Today it is widely considered a classic.

28   *So . . . for Alonzo there was an end to Hate called Death . . . and for Nanon, an end to Hate . . . called Love.* The Unknown, directed by Tod Browning (1927; Beverly Hills, CA: Metro-Goldwyn-Mayer, 2018), DVD. Before becoming

a filmmaker, Browning performed in circuses, sideshows, and vaudeville acts for thirteen years, working alternatively as a barker, contortionist, clown, magician's assistant, escape artist, singer, dancer, and blackface comedian.

32 ***The work of salvation*** . . . Gerrit Hohendorf, "The Extermination of Mentally Ill and Handicapped People under National Socialist Rule," *Mass Violence & Résistance*, November 17, 2016, https://www.sciencespo.fr/mass-violence -war-massacre-resistance/en/document/extermination -mentally-ill-and-handicapped-people-under-national -socialist-rule.html. For the Nazi doctors, killing and healing were not necessarily diametric opposites. Money saved through euthanizing incurably ill patients could be put toward treating those who stood a chance of recovery through modern methods—namely, electroconvulsive, insulin coma, and pentylenetetrazol therapies—or the most mutually beneficial and productive regimen, work therapy.

33 **In San Francisco, it was declared illegal for *any person who is diseased, maimed, mutilated or deformed in any way, so as to be an unsightly or disgusting object, to expose himself or herself to the public.*** City of San Francisco, "Order No. 783, To Prohibit Street Begging, and to Restrain Certain Persons from Appearing in Streets and Public Places," July 9, 1867. This ordinance from San Francisco is the earliest example of an ugly law known to researchers and stemmed from a general order to prohibit street begging. These reforms were led by the "Vigilance Committee," comprising wealthy businessmen who, according to the scholar Clare Sears, sought to target "offenses against good morals and decency."

33 **The last documented arrest made for an ugly law violation occurred in 1974.** Susan M. Schweik, *The Ugly Laws: Disability in Public* (New York: New York University Press, 2010), 6. This final arrest of an "unsightly beggar" occurred in Omaha, Nebraska. That same year, disability rights activists also instigated the repeal of a similar law in Chicago, effectively ending the American ugly laws.

34 **The special effects are realistic enough to convince Charlie Sheen he has watched a snuff film.** Tomo Kosuga, "Flowers of Flesh and Blood," *VICE*, September 30, 2009, https://www.vice.com/en/article/jmgkgg/flowers-of-flesh-and-blood. Tsutomu Miyazaki, in fact, owned a copy of *Guinea Pig 4: Devil Woman Doctor*, not *Guinea Pig 2*. Police misreported this finding to the press, spurring a moral panic around the influence of violent films and wrongfully attributing director Hideshi Hino with inspiring Miyazaki's crimes.

35 **. . . (sixty thousand reichsmark for a single cripple).** "Poster Promoting the Nazi Monthly Publication *Neues Volk*," *Holocaust Encyclopedia*, United States Holocaust Memorial Museum, https://encyclopedia.ushmm.org/content/en/photo/poster-promoting-the-nazi-monthly-publication-neues-volk. From a propaganda poster published by *Neues Volk* (New People), an Office of Racial Policy publication in Nazi Germany. The poster features an illustration of a disabled man seated in a chair with a smiling doctor standing behind him. The accompanying text is translated as, "This hereditarily ill person will cost our national community 60,000 Reichmarks over the course of his lifetime. Citizen, this is your money."

35 **Ironically, Minister of Propaganda Joseph Goebbels was himself disabled.** Peter Longerich, *Goebbels: A Biography* (New York: Random House, 2015), 5–6. Doctors diagnosed a young Goebbels as "foot lame for life," most likely a case of neurogenic clubfoot. Goebbels described his childhood as "pretty blighted," and as a result of his disability, he became withdrawn from his schoolmates. In 1919, he wrote a fictionalized account of his adolescence, *Michael Voormann's Early Years*, in which he explained his ambition as a way of compensating for his deformity.

37 **Of the remaining 1 percent on those lower floors who weren't so lucky, a high proportion were wheelchair users.** Glenn Corbett, "How the Design of the World Trade Center Claimed Lives on 9/11," *History*, September 10, 2018 (updated July 14, 2023), https://www.history.com/news/world-trade-center-stairwell-design-9-11. Firefighters from Ladder Company 6 encountered a disabled woman on stair B of the North Tower. As they carried her down the last few stories, the building collapsed. They later emerged from the rubble, the only group to be found alive in the stairwells after the tower came down.

37 **A blind man named Michael Hingson escaped the North Tower with the aid of his guide dog Roselle.** Michael Hingson with Susy Flory, *Thunder Dog: The True Story of a Blind Man, His Guide Dog, and the Triumph of Trust at Ground Zero* (New York: HarperCollins, 2011). Hingson was born blind but led a fruitful career as a businessman. At the time of the 9/11 attacks, he served as a regional sales manager and head of operations for a data-protection agency. Today, Hingson travels the country as a motivational speaker and advocate for people with visual impairments. His guide dog, Roselle, died in 2011.

38 **The Nazis based their own Law for the Prevention of Hereditarily Diseased Offspring on this original statute, the Model Eugenical Sterilization Law, and admired Laughlin enough to award him an honorary doctorate from Heidelberg University in 1936.** Harry Bruinius, *Better for All the World: The Secret History of Forced Sterilization and America's Quest for Racial Purity* (New York: Vintage, 2007), 316. Though the law was a holdover from the Weimar Republic, the Nazis embraced it heartily, sterilizing more than four hundred thousand people by the war's end. In a letter of thanks to Heidelberg University, Harry Laughlin wrote, "To me this honor will be doubly valued because it will come from a nation which for many centuries nurtured the human seed-stock which later founded my own country and thus gave basic character to our present lives and institutions." Paul A. Lombardo, a professor of law at Georgia State University who researched *Buck v. Bell* for twenty-five years, described Laughlin as "among the most racist and anti-Semitic of early twentieth-century eugenicists." To this day, the Supreme Court has not overturned *Buck v. Bell*

39 **Today, disabled children are twice as likely to experience physical or sexual violence and neglect.** Zuyi Fang, Ilan Cerna-Turoff, Cheng Zhang, Mengyao Lu, Jamie M Lachman, and Jane Barlow, "Global Estimates of Violence against Children with Disabilities: An Updated Systematic Review and Meta-Analysis," *The Lancet Child & Adolescent Health* 6, no. 5 (May 2022): 313–23. The study involved more than sixteen million children from twenty-five countries and analyzed data collected between 1990 and 2020. It found that 31.7 percent of disabled children surveyed had experienced some form of violence and that "the overall

odds ratio of children with versus without disabilities experiencing violence was 2·08."

40   ***In deformity and bodily disfigurement, there is good material for making jokes.*** Robert Garland, *The Eye of the Beholder: Deformity and Disability in the Graeco-Roman World* (London: Bristol Classical Press, 2010), 76. Cicero's own father was disabled. A wealthy member of the equestrian order, he was well connected but, as a cripple, unable to participate in public life.

42   ***. . . to retain something from him.*** The quotations attributed to Tsutomu Miyazaki used in this work should be considered apocryphal, as they lack reliable primary sources, although they are widely available online. I have omitted citations for these quotes from the notes section.

47   ***How she got that way will never be known.*** Browning, *Freaks.* The carnival barker's ambiguity is a common tactic among the so-called sideshow spielers, letting the audience's imagination embellish the backstory for whatever "freak" they may encounter.

48   ***I'll take all night if I have to.*** William M. Welch, "Disabled Climb Capitol Steps to Plea for Government Protection," Associated Press, March 12, 1990. Before participating in the Capitol Crawl, Jennifer Keelan and her mother were arrested during another protest in Montreal, when Keelan was only seven. She continues to work as a disability rights activist to this day.

48   **Nazi doctors preserved hundreds of disabled children's brains in jars . . .** Steven Erlanger, "Vienna Buries Child Victims of the Nazis," *New York Times*, April 29, 2002,

https://www.nytimes.com/2002/04/29/world/vienna
-buries-child-victims-of-the-nazis.html. Nazi neuroscien-
tists harvested thousands of brains from T4 victims. One
of the most notorious collections was overseen by Heinrich
Gross, former director of the Am Spiegelgrund clinic. After
the war, Gross was tried for manslaughter, but his convic-
tion was overturned. He continued serving as a prominent
neurological expert, and his trove of brains poached from
murdered disabled children was employed in research as
late as 1997, when Gross's unsavory past was exposed.
He was accused of war crimes, only for his trial to be sus
pended after a diagnosis of dementia deemed him mentally
unfit. He lived to be ninety. What a mind.

III. Fiend without a Face

53 **An estimated 10 percent of Americans fall into this
category, myself included.** Andrew Solomon, "What Happens When You're Disabled but Nobody Can Tell," *New
York Times*, July 10, 2020, https://www.nytimes.com/2020
/07/10/style/invisible-disabilities.html. The term "invisible disability" covers a wide spectrum of physical, mental,
and neurological conditions. People may have a disability
and not even be aware, or in cases like my own, may experience feelings of impostor syndrome.

54 . . . *lame brat.* J. V. Hirschmann, "Lord Byron's Deformed
Foot: A Medical and Biographical Assessment," *Byron Journal*
48, no. 1 (2020): 57–70, http://muse.jhu.edu/article/758749.
Although Gordon instilled a love of literature in a young
Lord Byron, their relationship was strained and sometimes
volatile. Gordon was left impoverished after her husband,
"Mad Jack" Byron, squandered his wife's inheritance and
abandoned the family for France (where he died when his

son was only three years old). Gordon never remarried and devoted herself to funding Byron's education on her limited income. She spent her final years in Nottinghamshire, alone except for her servants, receiving letters from Byron during his grand tour through Europe while simultaneously dodging her son's creditors. She died in 1811, just as Byron was returning home.

55 **Some historians speculate she was born with spina bifida . . .** Valmantas Budrys, "Neurological Deficits in the Life and Works of Frida Kahlo," *European Neurology 55*, no. 1 (2006): 4–10, https://doi.org/10.1159/000091136. The American surgeon Leo Eloesser, whom Kahlo consulted and corresponded with throughout her life, diagnosed her with a congenital deformation of the spine (scoliosis) and a missing vertebral disk. Upon examining X-rays of Kahlo, he noted: "X-rays showed spina bifida, the decreased sensitivity in the lower part of her body was characteristically compatible with this disorder." Kahlo was never formally diagnosed with spina bifida.

55 *I must have full skirts and long, now that my sick leg is so ugly.* Julien Levy, *Memoir of an Art Gallery* (New York: Putnam, 1977), 16. Kahlo also disguised her leg by wearing multiple pairs of socks and bandages. Her childhood experience with polio is reflected in the 1938 painting *They Ask for Planes and Only Get Straw Wings.*

56 **The Social Security Administration, though, flags fewer than 1 percent of disability claims as fraudulent.** Social Security Administration, "The Faces and Facts of Disability," https://www.ssa.gov/disabilityfacts/facts .html. This is in no small part due to the Cooperative Disability Investigations program, which examines suspicious claims before disability benefits are awarded.

56 **A mere 4 percent of the American working age population claim disability benefits.** The Social Security Administration, "Annual Statistical Report on the Social Security Disability Insurance Program, 2021," https://www.ssa.gov/policy/docs/statcomps/di_asr/2021/sect01.html. Being forced to continually prove one's disability while navigating a deliberately burdensome administrative infrastructure has a dehumanizing effect. These systemic challenges discourage people from seeking help, and the overall lack of a basic social safety net in the United States is, in my view, an utter disgrace.

56 **Meanwhile, the average American has a one in three chance of dying or becoming disabled before retirement.** Social Security Administration, "The Faces and Facts of Disability," https://www.ssa.gov/disabilityfacts/facts.html. Legalese makes qualifying for workers' compensation likewise difficult. One might be hurt at their place of employment, but if the injury does not arise from the work itself, loopholes can easily block any hope of a payout.

56 **In 2015, a Philadelphia woman named Linda Weston pled guilty to 196 criminal counts** . . . Jeremy Roebuck, "Life Deal for Woman Who Enslaved Disabled Adults in Tacony Basement," *Philadelphia Inquirer*, September 9, 2105, https://www.inquirer.com/philly/news/20150910_Life_deal_for_woman_who_enslaved_disabled_adults_in_Tacony_basement.html. Weston's attorneys claimed that their defendant had herself suffered physical and sexual abuse as a child, and during her testimony, Weston stated that she has depression and schizophrenia.

58 **The German watchmaker Stephan Farffler, a paraplegic, created the first self-propelled wheelchair in 1655.** Herman L. Kamenetz, "A Brief History of the Wheelchair,"

Journal of the History of Medicine and Allied Sciences 24, no. 2 (April 1969): 205–10, https://www.jstor.org/stable /24621915. A Chinese stone sculpture carved around 525 C.E. is perhaps the oldest known representation of a wheeled chair. For centuries, palanquins or litters were the preferred method of transportation for cripples.

58 *It is unbearable to me that the flower of our youth must lose their lives at the front, while that feeble-minded and asocial element can have a secure existence in the asylum.* Gerhard Schmidt, *Selektion in der Heilanstalt 1939– 1945 (Selection in the Mental Hospital 1939–1945)*, trans. Frank Schneider (Stuttgart, Germany: Evangelisches Verlagswerk, 1965), 34. An avowed Nazi and eugenicist, Pfannmuller oversaw the killing of at least three thousand disabled patients, including more than three hundred children, many of whom he personally injected with luminal or scopolamine-morphine. At the Nuremberg trials, he was sentenced to only five years in prison. Pfannmüller lived to be nearly seventy-five and died in 1961.

62 *. . . for as nature hath done ill by them, so do they by nature; being for the most part (as the Scripture saith) void of natural affection; and so they have their revenge of nature.* Francis Bacon, "On Deformity," in *The Essays of Francis Bacon*, ed. Mary Augusta Scott (New York: Scribner's, 1908), 200. Bacon's reasoning is most likely a consequence of the "argument from design," which posits that symmetry is a deliberate part of material creation and God's plan. Anything asymmetrical, such as cripples, must then be accidental or the product of transgression. The philosopher David Hume considers the opposite in *Dialogues Concerning Natural Religion*, proposing that since the universe is imperfect, its creator may have been a defective.

62 *I am determined to prove a villain / And hate the idle pleasures of these days.* William Shakespeare, *King Richard III*, ed. Janis Lull (Cambridge: Cambridge University Press, 2009), 290. When the real Richard III's body was exhumed after being discovered beneath a parking lot in Leicester in 2012, his skeleton was found to show signs of severe scoliosis.

63 *Chloroform unfit children.* Clarence Darrow, "Noted Men and Women Differ on Ethics of Letting Baby Die," *Washington Post*, November 18, 1915, 7. Darrow is referencing the infamous case of "Baby Bollinger," who was born in Chicago on November 12, 1915, with abnormal skin development. The infant, named John, died five days later, after the attending physician, Harry Haiselden, opted not to perform surgery on eugenical grounds. As part of an extensive publicity campaign to defend his actions, Haiselden wrote and starred in the 1917 film *The Black Stork*, in which he plays the benevolent Dr. Dickey, who refuses to operate on a disabled baby. The child is saved by another doctor, only to grow into a "monstrosity," seeking vengeance on those who condemned him to life. Back in the real world, Haiselden was tried and acquitted for the death of John Bollinger and was even permitted to keep his medical license. In total, he was responsible for the deaths of three infants. Two years after his film debut, Haiselden died of a cerebral hemorrhage while vacationing in Cuba, aged forty-nine.

64 **A 530,000-year-old deformed skull discovered in a Spanish cave suggests that early hominids were capable of caring for disabled kin.** Amy Barth, "Humans Took Care of the Disabled over 500,000 Years Ago," *Discover Magazine*, December 21, 2009, https://www.discovermagazine

.com/planet-earth/82-humans-took-care-of-the-disabled
-over-500-000-years-ago. One of the paleoanthropologists
who published an analysis of "Cranium 14" notes that this
particular find stood out because it is not uncommon for
mammals to kill burdensome offspring.

66 *I wanted to cry when I saw them.* John Kobal, *People Will
Talk* (New York: Knopf, 1986), 52. Baclanova also starred in
the 1928 silent film *The Man Who Laughs,* in which she is
simultaneously aroused and appalled by the protagonist's
disfigured face.

66 **The ancient Egyptians are credited with designing the
first artificial limb.** Jason Daley, "This 3,000-Year-Old
Wooden Toe Shows Early Artistry of Prosthetics," *Smithsonian Magazine,* June 21, 2017, https://www.smithsonianmag
.com/smart-news/study-reveals-secrets-ancient-cairo
-toe-180963783. Known as the "Cairo Toe," the prosthesis
belonged to a woman, possibly the daughter of a high-
ranking priest. Researchers found that the wooden toe had
been meticulously refitted several times to better match the
woman's foot.

66 **When she was only twenty-one, the American performance artist Lisa Bufano had her lower legs and most
of her fingers amputated . . .** Andrea Shea, "Remembering
Lisa Bufano, A Dancer Who Found Beauty in Amputation,"
WBUR, December 24, 2013, https://www.wbur.org/news
/2013/12/24/lisa-bufano-remembrance. Bufano begins *Five
Open Mouths* wearing carbon fiber legs but eventually sheds
the prosthetics in a stunning display of vulnerability. A
recording of the performance can be viewed through the
NYU library archives at https://sites.dlib.nyu.edu/hidvl
/6t1g1s68.

68 ***Here are some more coming to be gassed!*** Gitta Sereny, *Into That Darkness: An Examination of Conscience* (New York: Vintage, 1983), 97. From a letter written by the County Court in Frankfurt to Minister of Justice Gürtner, dated May 16, 1941.

69 ***Despite my own terror and discomfort in being watched* . . .** Amanda Cachia, "The Praying Mantis, the Exquisite Corpse, and Lisa Bufano," in *Disability and Art History*, ed. Ann Millett-Gallant and Elizabeth Howie (Oxfordshire: Routledge, 2016), 138. From an artist statement titled "Persistence of Vision" written in 2007 by Bufano.

69 ***Like a sword through a bull* . . .** Raquel Tibol, *Frida Kahlo: An Open Life*, trans. Elinor Randall (Albuquerque: University of New Mexico Press, 1993), 43. Recalling the accident and her impalement, Kahlo later joked, "I lost my virginity."

70 ***Who sinned, this man or his parents, that he was born blind?*** John 9:1-5.

70 ***I do not doubt there is far more in trivialities* . . .** Walt Whitman, "Faith Poem," in *Walt Whitman: Selected Poems 1855–1892*, ed. Gary Schmidgall (New York: St. Martin's Griffin, 1999), 153–54. Whitman's fervent nationalism was a paradoxical vision of egalitarian democracy that discounted Native Americans, African Americans, immigrants, and cripples alike.

72 ***Our puny sentimentalism has caused us to forget* . . .** Helen Keller, "Physicians' Juries for Defective Babies," *New Republic*, December 18, 1915, 173–74. Like Clarence Darrow, Keller is referencing "Baby Bollinger." She seems to have later renounced some of her support for eugenics, publicly

arguing for a life-saving surgery to be performed on a baby born with a rare eye disease in 1938. Still, throughout her life, Keller distanced herself from disability rights groups.

74 ***Goya gives thanks to his friend Arrieta*** . . . Gretchen Halverson, "Goya's Gratitude and the Long Tradition of Artistic Tributes to Health Workers," Minneapolis Institute of Art, March 31, 2020, https://new.artsmia.org/stories/goyas -gratitude-and-the-long-tradition-of-artistic-tributes-to -health-workers. From the original Spanish, "Goya agradecido, á su amigo Arrieta: por el acierto y esmero con q.e le salvó la vida en su agúda y- peligrosa enfermedad, padecido á fines de año 1819, a los setenta y tres años de su edad. Lo pintó en 1820." Not long after treating Goya, Eugenio García Arrieta is believed to have left Spain to study bubonic plague in Africa, where he presumably died.

75 . . . ***people who are smashed getting smashed.*** Vivien Goldman, "Up from Rock Bottom," *Melody Maker*, March 15, 1980. While interviewing Wyatt, Goldman suggests the singer should get an "invalid car," to which Wyatt's wife, Alfie, replies, "No, not Robert, he's a born passenger . . ."

76 ***It's okay . . . It's okay . . . I'm a friend . . . I won't hurt you . . . Come on . . . Wait . . . Wait.*** Dialogue from the film *Don't Look Now*, directed by Nicolas Roeg (1973; New York: Criterion Collection, 2015), DVD.

IV. How to Make a Monster

80 **The four-thousand-year-old remains of a crippled man were discovered at the Neolithic archaeological site Mán Bạc** . . . Andrew Curry, "Ancient Bones Offer Clues to How Long Ago Humans Cared for the Vulnerable,"

NPR, June 17, 2020. https://www.kpbs.org/news/2020/06/17/ancient-bones-offer-clues-to-how-long-ago-humans. Lorna Tilley, an Australian archaeologist who helped uncover Burial 9, has developed a concept she calls the "bio-archaeology of care," a means to understand past societies through studying the ways in which sick and disabled people were cared for.

80 *Because I think he's simply a mass of flesh without a soul.* Martin Luther, *Luther's Works*, vol. 54, ed. J. Pelikan and H. T. Lehmann (Philadelphia: Fortress, 1967), 397. In his later years, Martin Luther experienced significant physical decline, suffering from vertigo, tinnitus, fainting spells, cataracts, kidney and bladder stones, arthritis, a ruptured eardrum, and chest pains. A stroke killed him in 1546, at age sixty-two. The devil's work, indeed.

81 *And now the fifth commandment: "Thou shalt not kill," is set aside and broken . . .* Hohendorf, "The Extermination of Mentally Ill and Handicapped People under National Socialist Rule." From "Sermon of the Bishop Clemens Graf von Galen in the Lambertikirche in Münster, August 3, 1941." Galen's anti-euthanasia sermons were printed and distributed illegally; thousands of these pamphlets were circulated throughout Germany, garnering popular opposition against the T4 program. Hitler wanted Galen removed as bishop, and other Nazi officials suggested he should be assassinated, but Joseph Goebbels cautioned that the backlash would be too severe. Galen was effectively kept under house arrest until the war's end. He later became a cardinal and was beatified after his death.

83 **Nine percent of white workers report having disabilities, compared to 11 percent of Black workers.** Martha Ross and Nicole Bateman, "Disability Rates among

Working-Age Adults Are Shaped by Race, Place, and Education," Brookings Institution, May 15, 2018, https://www.brookings.edu/articles/disability-rates-among-working-age-adults-are-shaped-by-race-place-and-education. Native Americans account for the highest disability rate among working-age adults, at 16 percent.

85 ***Love led the two of us to one death.*** Dante Alighieri, "Canto V," l. 106, in *Inferno*, trans. Allen Mandelbaum (New York: Bantam, 1982), 45. Dante may have met Paolo Malatesta as a youth in Florence. He also lived with Francesca's nephew, Guido Novello da Polento, in Ravenna toward the end of his life.

86 ***. . . a spiritual automobile accident.*** Arthur Lubow, *Diane Arbus: Portrait of a Photographer* (New York: Ecco, 2016), 216. From a letter written by Diane Arbus to Pati Hill, n d. [May 1957], Pati Hill Collection.

87 ***I firmly believe that a government that forbids killing among its citizens should not be in the business of killing people itself.*** Larry Flynt, "Don't Execute the Man Who Paralyzed Me (Guest Column)," *Hollywood Reporter*, October 17, 2013, https://www.hollywoodreporter.com/news/general-news/larry-flynt-dont-execute-man-649158. Although stating he does not want to kill his shooter, Flynt admits that he would enjoy an hour alone in a room with Franklin and a pair of wire cutters.

87 **Disability rights activist Stella Young coined the phrase *inspiration porn* . . .** Stella Young, "I'm Not Your Inspiration, Thank You Very Much," filmed June 9, 2014, in Sydney, Australia. TED video, 8:47, https://www.ted.com/talks/stella_young_i_m_not_your_inspiration_thank_you_very_much. Young, who uses a wheelchair,

explains, "People, when they say, 'You're an inspiration,' they mean it as a compliment. And I know why it happens. It's because of the lie. It's because we've been sold this lie that disability makes you exceptional. And it honestly doesn't."

89 *Groovy.* Dialogue from the film *Evil Dead II*, directed by Sam Raimi (1987; Santa Monica, CA: Lionsgate, 2011), DVD.

94 *A horse, a horse, my kingdom for a horse!* Shakespeare, *King Richard III.* Richard III's famous plea from act 5, scene 4.

94 **Only 21 percent of disabled Americans are currently employed.** "Persons with a Disability: Labor Force Characteristics—2022," Bureau of Labor Statistics, February 23, 2023, https://www.bls.gov/news.release/pdf/disabl.pdf. It is also worth noting that people with disabilities are far less likely to have completed bachelor's degrees or higher than their able-bodied peers.

95 *. . . so people could get to eat in the commissary without throwing up.* Skal and Savada, *Dark Carnival,* 168. Anecdotally, F. Scott Fitzgerald, while working as a screenwriter for MGM, is said to have dined in the aforementioned commissary alongside the conjoined twins Daisy and Violet Hilton, which is recounted in his story "Crazy Sunday."

96 **After the death of her lover Gertrude Lawrence . . .** Peter Bradshaw, "Don't Look Now and Roeg's Red Coat," *The Guardian,* January 18, 2011, https://www.theguardian.com/film/2011/jan/18/dont-look-now-red-coat. There is some controversy surrounding claims that du Maurier had relationships with other women. She was married to a man for more than thirty years and had three children, but still, rumors persist. Her biographer, Margaret Forster, has implied du Maurier was a repressed bisexual.

97   *Artifacts of a bygone era* . . . Dialogue from the film *The Fly*, directed by David Cronenberg (1986; Los Angeles: 20th Century Fox, 2014), Blu-ray.

98   *I want to be seen as attractive and beautiful and sexy like everyone else.* Andrea Shea, "Artist Takes Inspiration from Amputation," NPR, March 19, 2007, https://www.npr .org/2007/03/19/7728628/artist-takes-inspiration-from -amputation. As a tribute to the film *Freaks*, Bufano tattooed the phrase "One of us" on her right hand.

99   *Like us* . . . Dialogue from the film *A Zed & Two Noughts*, directed by Peter Greenaway (1985; New York: Zeitgeist Films, 2008), DVD.

100   **She posed nude as a means of reconnecting with her own sexuality** . . . Chet Cooper, "Playboy Interview: Hugh Hefner and Playmate Ellen Stohl Talk with Chet Cooper," *Ability Magazine*, 1995, https://abilitymagazine.com /charles-Hugh%20Hefner-stohl.html. In reflecting on the photo shoot, Stohl explains that she wanted to be seen as a woman, not a wheelchair, and that her life's story has been about more than overcoming tragedy.

V. The Damned

105   *Doctor, here is business enough for you.* Henry Jacob Bigelow, "Dr. Harlow's Case of Recovery from the Passage of an Iron Bar through the Head," *American Journal of the Medical Sciences* 20, no. 39 (1850): 16. Upon initial examination, doctors were incredulous that an iron rod had actually passed through Gage's head, until an Irish itinerant worker said, "Sure it was so, sir, for the bar is lying in the road below, all blood and brains."

106   **This unlucky duo have their bodies boiled so the skeletons can be exhibited in museums.** Yehuda Koren and
Eliat Negev, *In Our Hearts We Were Giants: The Remarkable
Story of the Lilliput Troupe* (Boston: Da Capo Press, 2004),
177. Mengele was fascinated with physical abnormalities
and, in addition to dwarfs, experimented on giants, hunchbacks, and twins. Hitler too was intrigued by dwarfism and
kept a private print of Disney's animated film *Snow White
and the Seven Dwarfs.*

106   **Pliny the Elder describes two giants, a male named
Pusio and a female named Secundilla.** Lisa Trentin,
"Deformity in the Roman Imperial Court," *Greece & Rome*
58, no. 2 (October 2011): 197, https://www.jstor.org/stable
/41306156. On the opposite end of the spectrum, Augustus also exhibited a dwarf named Lycius, who was less than
two feet tall.

108   ***God, I love you.*** Dialogue from the film *Misery,* directed
by Rob Reiner (1990; Beverly Hills, CA: Metro-Goldwyn-
Mayer, 2015), DVD.

110   **... *mad, bad, and dangerous to know.*** Paul Douglass, *Lady
Caroline Lamb: A Biography* (London: Palgrave Macmillan,
2004), 104. The most contemporary source claiming that
Lamb said this comes from the memoirs of her friend, Sydney, Lady Morgan. Like Byron, Lamb was also a writer, and
her gothic novel *Glenarvon* was praised by Goethe.

110   **And lest we forget Byron's Scottish nanny May Gray ...**
Benita Eisley, *Byron: Child of Passion, Fool of Fame* (New
York: Knopf, 2000), 39. Purportedly a religious fanatic,
Gray both sexually and physically abused Byron. She is also
said to have terrified Byron by telling him ghost stories and
locking him in unlit rooms.

111 *He is fitful, irreverent, indulging at times in the grossest profanity* . . . John M. Harlow, *Recovery from the Passage of an Iron Bar through the Head* (Boston: Clapp, 1869), 13. Gage's shift in personality may have been temporary (and exaggerated), as Harlow's account followed shortly after the accident. Gage later traveled to Chile, where he worked as a stagecoach driver for several years before his death and was described as being mentally sound.

111 . . . *off the fatta the lan'.* John Steinbeck, *Of Mice and Men* (New York: Penguin, 1994), 15. Lennie's intellectual disability is never explicitly named. George simply refers to him as "dumb" but insists Lennie is not "crazy."

112 **Between 2011 and 2015, at least 219 disabled people were killed by their parents or caregivers** . . . David Perry, "Media Coverage of the Murder of People with Disabilities by Their Caregivers," Ruderman Family Foundation, March 2017, https://rudermanfoundation.org/white_papers /media-coverage-of-the-murder-of-people-with-disabilities -by-their-caregivers. In this study, a plurality of victims had multiple disabilities, with "hardship" most frequently cited as motivation for the killings.

114 *I'm next or I shoot you. Dinner with Henry,* directed by Richard Young (1979; Big Sur, CA: the Henry Miller Memorial Library, 1984), VHS, https://www.ubu.com/film /miller_dinner.html. Dialogue from a short documentary featuring Henry Miller dining with Brenda Venus, who recounts the filming in her 1986 book *Dear, Dear Brenda: The Love Letters of Henry Miller.* Miller was asked to discuss wine but instead spoke freely on a variety of topics, chiefly his friend Blaise Cendrars.

114 **In World War I, military doctors often relied on guillotines to perform quick amputations.** Julie Anderson, "Wounding in World War One," *British Library*, January 29, 2014, https://www.bl.uk/world-war-one/articles/wounding-in-world-war-one. Also known as "flapless amputations," this method was particularly effective in removing gangrenous limbs, with the clean cut allowing for better drainage and thus increasing the likelihood of survival.

115 *Nothing remains, nothing lasts, except this longstanding pain in my severed arm . . .* Laurent Tatu, Julien Bogousslavsky, and François Boller, "Phantoms in Artists: The Lost Limbs of Blaise Cendrars, Arthur Rimbaud, and Paul Wittgenstein," *Journal of the History of the Neurosciences* 23, no. 4 (2014), 360, https://doi.org/10.1080/0964704x.2014.881168. Excerpted from "Memento 1953–1958," Blaise Cendrars Collection, Swiss National Library, Bern, 1956.

117 *. . . constant companion.* Harlow, "Recovery from the Passage of an Iron Bar through the Head," 340. Gage's mother later sent her son's skull to Harlow in the name of science. Today, it is on display at the Warren Anatomical Museum in Boston.

118 *Who will survive and what will be left of them?* Original tagline from the film *The Texas Chain Saw Massacre*, directed by Tobe Hooper (1974; Orland Park, IL: Dark Sky Films, 2014), Blu-ray.

118 *The disabled can only create misery . . .* Arata Yamamoto, "Japan Alleged Mass Murderer: 'All Disabled Should Cease to Exist,'" *NBC News*, July 26, 2016, https://www.nbcnews.com/news/world/japan-alleged-mass-murderer-all-disabled-should-cease-exist-n616791. From a letter written

by Satoshi Uematsu to Tadamori Oshima, February 15, 2016.

121 ... *who have no calves, or are weasel-armed, or have three eyes, or ostrich-heads* ... Plutarch, "De Curiositate," in *Moralia*, trans. W. C. Helmbold (Cambridge, MA: Harvard University Press, 1939), 499. Roman emperors were especially fond of people with disabilities. Commodus, for instance, once served guests at a private banquet two fully cooked hunchbacks smeared with mustard—on a silver platter, no less.

121 **Judy Garland claimed she was often groped while filming with the Munchkins** ... Matt Weinstock, "'The Wizard of Oz,' the Last Munchkin, and the Little People Left Behind," *New Yorker*, July 11, 2018, https://www.newyorker.com/culture/culture-desk/the-wizard-of-oz-the-last-munchkin-and-the-little-people-left-behind. Garland proliferated many of these rumors, most notably in a 1967 interview with Jack Paar; however, most of this salacious gossip has been debunked in Aljean Harmetz's book, *The Making of "The Wizard of Oz."*

122 *Mein Führer, I can walk!* Dialogue from the film *Dr. Strangelove or: How I Learned to Stop Worrying and Love the Bomb*, directed by Stanley Kubrick (1964; New York: Criterion Collection, 2020), DVD.

125 *We represent the Lollipop Guild, the Lollipop Guild, the Lollipop Guild!* Lyrics from the song by Harold Arlen and Edgar Yipsel, "The Lollipop Guild," in *The Wizard of Oz*, directed by Victor Fleming (1939; Beverly Hills, CA: Metro-Goldwyn-Mayer, 2013), DVD.

125 *And on behalf of the Lollipop Guild, we'd like to welcome you to Munchkinland!* Arlen and Yipsel, "The Lollipop Guild."

125 *Follow the yellow brick road!* Lyrics from the song by Harold Arlen and Edgar Yipsel, "Follow the Yellow Brick Road / You're Off to See the Wizard," in *The Wizard of Oz*, directed by Victor Fleming (1939; Beverly Hills, CA: Metro-Goldwyn-Mayer, 2013), DVD.

128 *Les femmes soignent ces féroces infirmes retour des pays chauds.* Arthur Rimbaud, "Bad Blood," in *A Season in Hell*, trans. Louise Varèse (New York: New Directions, 2011), 12–13. In English: "Women nurse those fierce invalids, home from hot countries."

129 *My eye has always been drawn to abnormal forms.* Ginger Murray, "Performance Artist Lisa Bufano: In Remembrance," *SF Weekly*, October 28, 2013. Bufano also had a fascination with costumes that accentuated her amputations and created custom outfits for photo shoots, including a squid, mermaid, and doll.

132 *I drank because I wanted to drown my sorrows, but now the damned things have learned to swim.* Hayden Harrera, *Frida: The Biography of Frida Kahlo* (New York: HarperCollins, 1983), 438. From a letter written by Frida Kahlo to Ella Wolfe, dated "Wednesday 13," [1938].

136 **An estimated 420,000 disabled workers in America receive an average wage of $2.15 per hour.** Sarah Kim, "The Truth of Disability Employment That No One Talks About," *Forbes*, October 24, 2019, https://www.forbes.com/sites/sarahkim/2019/10/24/sub-minimum-wages-disability/?sh=738cebefc22b. In 2018, the ten largest

"sheltered workshops" employing people with disabilities had a combined annual revenue of $523 million, with one CEO earning $1.1 million per year.

137 ***Your pussy looks delicious.*** Priscilla Frank, "Chuck Close Is a Giant of the Art World: He's Allegedly Also a 'F**king Pervert,'" *Huffington Post*, December 19, 2017, https:// www.huffpost.com/entry/chuck-close-sexual-harassment _n_59f877dee4b09b5c2568fd88. Lance Gotko, one of Close's lawyers, responded to the *Huffington Post* investigation by claiming that "if the article has its intended effect *it will literally kill Mr. Close.*"

139 **. . . *getting out was a lot more difficult than jumping in.*** Werner Herzog, "Blasphemy and Mirages," in *Herzog on Herzog*, ed. Paul Cronin (London: Faber and Faber, 2002), 58. Herzog's film was the first to utilize an entire cast of dwarf actors since the 1938 western *The Terror of Tiny Town.*

VI. Terror Is a Man

144 ***Where's that squealin' son of yours?*** Dialogue from the film *Kiss of Death*, directed by Henry Hathaway (1947; Los Angeles: 20th Century Fox, 2005), DVD.

146 ***Vietnam.*** Stacy Jenel Smith, "Jade Calegory Has Eye Set on Out-of-This-World Career," *Los Angeles Times*, August 23, 1988, https://www.latimes.com/archives/la-xpm-1988-08 -23-ca-842-story.html. Calegory appeared only in one other made-for-TV movie after the release of *Mac and Me*. Today, he works as a photographer.

148   *... crippled in body and soul, miserable wretches, a burden to both themselves and to others* ... Dialogue from the film *Dasein ohne Leben—Psychiatrie und Menschlichkeit* (*Existence Without Life—Psychiatry and Humanity*), directed by Hermann Schwenninger (1942; Berlin: Tobis Film), Steven Spielberg Film and Video Archive.

148   *... modus operandi: montage, collage, bricolage.* Hob Broun, "Highspeed Linear Main St.," in *Cardinal Numbers* (New York: Knopf, 1988), 78. This collection of stories was released posthumously.

150   *... punishment.* Hayden Herrera, "Frida Kahlo: The Palette, the Pain, and the Painter," *Artforum*, March 1983, https://www.artforum.com/print/198303/frida-kahlo-the -palette-the-pain-and-the-painter-35514. In her 1944 painting *The Broken Column*, Kahlo can be seen wearing one of these corsets, her body split open down the middle, revealing a damaged ionic column in place of her spine, dozens of nails embedded in her flesh, tear-filled eyes betraying her stoic expression.

151   *... the science of the improvement of the human race by better breeding.* Charles Davenport, *Eugenics: The Science of Human Improvement by Better Breeding* (New York: Henry Holt, 1910). Davenport kept ties with the Nazis before and during World War II and held editorial positions at two German journals. As founder of the International Federation of Eugenics Organizations, he was particularly troubled by interracial relationships and was a staunch anti-immigration advocate.

152   *Sanctuary! Sanctuary!* Victor Hugo, *The Hunchback of Notre Dame* (Ware: Wordsworth Classics, 1998), 298. Quasimodo's famous cry.

153 ***I'm scared of you sometimes, of how you snap at me.*** Richard Allen Green, "Reeva to Oscar Pistorius: 'I'm Scared of You Sometimes,'" CNN, March 24, 2014, https://www.cnn.com/2014/03/24/world/africa/south-africa-pistorius-trial/index.html. During her final year of studying law, Steenkamp broke her back in a horseback riding accident and was temporarily paralyzed. She had to relearn how to walk before making a full recovery.

153 **Surveys suggest that around two-thirds of the able-bodied population feel uncomfortable around disabled persons.** "Brits Feel Uncomfortable with Disabled People," *Scope*, May 8, 2014, https://www.scope.org.uk/media/press-releases/brits-feel-uncomfortable-with-disabled-people. This UK-based survey also found that nearly half of respondents did not personally know someone with a disability.

155 ***For the task of an artist, blindness is not a total misfortune.*** Jorge Luis Borges, "Blindness," in *Selected Non-Fictions* (New York: Viking, 1999), 482. Borges referred to his blindness as "modest" because he could still make out certain colors, most prominently yellow.

158 ***Mentally dead . . . human ballast . . . empty shells of human beings.*** Robert Jay Lifton, "German Doctors and the Final Solution," *New York Times*, September 21, 1986, 64. Alfred Hoche, professor of psychiatry at the University of Freiburg and coauthor of the influential *Die Freigabe der Vernichtung lebensunwerten Lebens* (*The Permission to Destroy Life Unworthy of Life*), argued that euthanizing disabled patients should not be equated with other types of killing and described the practice as "an allowable, useful act."

160 ***The solution of the problem of the mentally ill becomes
easy if one eliminates these people.*** Robert Jay Lifton, *The
Nazi Doctors: Medical Killing and the Psychology of Genocide*
(New York: Macmillan, 1986), 50. From Otto Mauthe's testimony during the Heyde trial, December 20, 1961, 42–43.

161 ***If we hadn't a voice or a tongue, and wanted to express
things to one another*** . . . Plato, *Cratylus*, trans. C. D. C.
Reeve (Indianapolis: Hackett Publishing Company, 1998),
67. During this section of the dialogue, which is concerned
with language and the convention of naming, Socrates
suggests that if someone who lacks a voice wanted to communicate, they would be required to imitate the nature of a
particular thing, as in describing a horse by behaving like
one. He is asking whether language itself is merely a series
of arbitrary signs or if words have intrinsic relationships
with whatever they signify.

162 ***Ladies and gentlemen*** . . . ***brace yourselves up to witness
one who is probably the most remarkable human being
ever to draw the breath of life.*** Michael Howell and Peter
Ford, *The True History of the Elephant Man* (New York: Penguin, 2011), 148. Introductory speech for the Elephant Man
exhibition as spoken by Tom Norman, a showman who
served as Joseph Merrick's manager in Whitechapel.

164 *. . . **the most disgusting specimen of humanity that I had
ever seen*** . . . Frederick Treves, *The Elephant Man and Other
Reminisces* (London: Cassell and Co., 1923), 1. Treves worked
primarily as a surgeon, specializing in abdominal surgery,
and performed the first appendectomy in London. He later
served Queen Victoria as a "Surgeon Extraordinary" and is
credited with saving the life of Edward VII by treating his
appendicitis shortly before the coronation in 1902.

165 ***A man in the heyday of youth who was so vilely deformed that everyone he met confronted him with a look of horror and disgust*** . . . Treves, *The Elephant Man and Other Reminisces*, 3. Ironically, Treves himself died of peritonitis in 1923, likely the cause of a ruptured appendix.

166 ***Dear Miss Maturin*** . . . "'Elephant Man' Joseph Merrick letter in Leicester display," BBC, September 9, 2017, https://www.bbc.com/news/uk-england-leicestershire -41207179. From a letter written by Joseph Merrick to Leila Maturin, October 7, 1889.

167 ***He often said to me that he wished he could lie down to sleep "like other people"*** . . . Treves, *The Elephant Man and Other Reminisces*, 38. Treves performed the autopsy and concluded that Merrick died of a dislocated neck, which possibly severed an artery.

168 ***'Tis true, my form is something odd*** . . . Included in a pamphlet titled *The Elephant Man*, amplified from an account published in *British Medical Journal* 11 (December 11, 1886): 1188–89. Howell and Ford, *The True History of the Elephant Man*, 341.

VII. The Vengeance of the Flesh

172 ***It's really something*** . . . Raymond Carver, "Cathedral," in *Cathedral* (New York: Vintage, 1993), 228. At this moment of catharsis, the narrator, his eyes closed, acknowledges he is still inside his house, but at the same time, feels as if he is not inside anything at all.

172 ***People say it's a metaphor for some other thing*** . . . Raymond Carver, "Stories Don't Come Out of Thin Air," interview by Claude Grimal, trans. William L. Stull,

Clockwatch Review 10, nos. 1–2 (1996), 9–16. Carver considered "Cathedral" to be among his best stories and said it was completely different from anything he had previously written.

173 **Suicidal ideation is more prevalent among people with disabilities.** "Disparities in Suicide," Centers for Disease Control and Prevention, May 9, 2023, https://www.cdc.gov/suicide/facts/disparities-in-suicide.html. A 2021 survey found that adults with disabilities were three times more likely to report suicidal ideation in the past month than their able-bodied peers.

174 **Every year around twenty-five thousand Americans die or are permanently disabled from medical diagnostic errors.** Kaveh G. Shojania and Mary Dixon-Woods, "Estimating Deaths Due to Medical Error: The Ongoing Controversy and Why It Matters," *BMJ Quality & Safety* 26 (2017): 425, http://dx.doi.org/10.1136/bmjqs-2016-006144. This figure comes from a report criticizing the veracity of an earlier study, which estimated that more than 250,000 people die from medical diagnostic errors annually.

174 *Age 56–57.—For 25 years extreme spasmodic daily & nightly flatulence* . . . Charles Darwin, "Note to Dr. John Chapman—20 May 1865," in *The Correspondence of Charles Darwin*, vol. 13, *1865*, ed. Frederick Burkhardt and Sydney Smith (Cambridge: Cambridge University Press 1985), 482. Darwin was treated by at least twenty doctors, with little success. He blamed his digestive troubles on mental exertion: "I find the noddle & the stomach are antagonist powers," he wrote to his sister, "and that it is a great deal more easy to think too much in a day, than to think too little—What thought has to do with digesting roast beef,—I cannot say, but they are brother faculties."

175 **Twenty-seven percent of American military veterans report service-related disabilities.** "Employment Situation of Veterans—2022," Bureau of Labor Statistics, March 21, 2023, https://www.bls.gov/news.release/pdf/vet.pdf. This percentage accounts for 4.9 million veterans.

178 *Not the least hope remains to me . . . Everything moves in time with what the belly contains.* Herrera, "Frida Kahlo: The Palette, the Pain, and the Painter." The following year, in a letter written to a friend preceding her spinal surgery, Kahlo wrote, ". . . as a sick person I am rather stoic, but that now it is a little hard for me because in this fucking life, one suffers but one learns."

179 *. . . quite classic.* Arthur Lubow, "Arbus Reconsidered," *New York Times*, September 14, 2003, https://www.nytimes.com /2003/09/14/magazine/arbus-reconsidered.html. From a letter by Diane Arbus to Carlotta Marshall, late 1968.

182 **More than a quarter of chronically homeless people in the United States have a disability.** "The 2020 Annual Homeless Assessment Report (AHAR) to Congress," US Department of Housing and Urban Development, January 2021, 64, https://www.huduser.gov/portal/sites/default /files/pdf/2020-AHAR-Part-1.pdf. This report defines a chronically homeless person as "an individual with a disability who has been continuously homeless for one year or more or has experienced at least four episodes of homelessness in the last three years where the combined length of time homeless on those occasions is at least 12 months."

182 *I am such a strange mélange of good and evil that it would be difficult to describe me.* Lord Byron, *Lady Blessington's Conversations of Lord Byron*, ed. Ernest J. Lovell (Princeton, NJ: Princeton University Press, 1969), 220. Byron

elaborates, "I am of a wayward, uncertain disposition, more disposed to display the defects than the redeeming points in my nature: this, at least proves that I understand mankind, for they are always ready to believe the evil, but not the good."

184   **Between one-third and half of all people killed by police are disabled.** Marti Hause and Ari Melber, "Half of People Killed by Police Have a Disability: Report," *NBC News*, March 14, 2016, https://www.nbcnews.com/news /us-news/half-people-killed-police-suffer-mental-disability -report-n538371. The original report was published by the Ruderman Family Foundation and analyzed incidents of police violence from 2013 to 2015.

184   *. . . paint, paint, paint.* Rafael Lozano, "Mexico City Dispatch," *Time*, November 9, 1950. Kahlo continued to work during her convalescence, despite being instructed to avoid painting. In 1953, when Kahlo held her first solo exhibition in Mexico, doctors insisted she was too ill to attend. Undaunted, Kahlo arrived via ambulance and was carried into the gallery on a stretcher, where she was placed on a four-poster bed. While talking to reporters, she said, "I am not sick, I am broken. But I am happy to be alive as long as I can paint."

186   *Do not repent that with so high and pure a feeling . . .* Nathaniel Hawthorne, "The Birth-Mark," in *The Complete Novels and Selected Tales of Nathaniel Hawthorne* (New York: Random House, 1977), 1021–31. In his journal, Hawthorne wrote a preliminary sketch that served as the story's genesis: "A person to be the death of his beloved in trying to raise her to more than mortal perfection; yet this should be a comfort to him for having aimed so highly and holily."

187 *I saw the pale student of unhallowed arts kneeling beside the thing he had put together.* Mary Shelley, introduction to *Frankenstein* (London: Henry Colburn and Richard Bentley, 1831), x. Shelley initially published *Frankenstein* anonymously, and her insistence that writing the novel was "making only a transcript" of her dream may have served as a means of protection. She feared losing custody of her children as a result of controversy surrounding her book, which despite its popularity was described by one member of Parliament as a "tissue of horrible and disgusting absurdity."

188 *I was benevolent; my soul glowed with love and humanity . . .* Shelley, *Frankenstein*, 84. Shelley's mother, the feminist writer and philosopher Mary Wollstonecraft, wrote in *An Historical and Moral View of the Origin and Progress of the French Revolution* (1795), "People are rendered ferocious by misery; and misanthropy is ever the offspring of discontent."

189 *A Monster Science Created—But Could Not Destroy!* Original tagline from the film *Frankenstein*, directed by James Whale (1931; Universal City, CA: Universal Pictures, 2016), Blu-ray.

192 **More than a quarter of households in the United States with at least one disabled family member have medical debt.** Neil Bennett, Jonathan Eggleston, Laryssa Mykyta, and Briana Sullivan, "Who Had Medical Debt in the United States? 19% of US Households Could Not Afford to Pay for Medical Care Right Away," US Census Bureau, April 7, 2021, https://www.census.gov/library/stories/2021/04/who-had-medical-debt-in-united-states.html. Based on a US Census Bureau study conducted in 2017 and published in 2018.

193 ***Uhh! I don't know what I said! Uhhh! I don't remember!*** "Donald Trump Criticized for Mocking Disabled Reporter," *Snopes*, July 28, 2016, https://www.snopes.com /news/2016/07/28/donald-trump-criticized-for-mocking -disabled-reporter. Responding to the backlash, Trump claimed ignorance: "I have no idea who this reporter, Serge Kovalski [*sic*] is, what he looks like or his level of intelligence. . . . If Mr. Kovaleski is handicapped, I would not know because I do not know what he looks like. If I did know, I would definitely not say anything about his appearance." Kovaleski pointed out that, in fact, he had known Trump for years and interviewed him several times as a reporter for the *Daily News*.

198 ***I sometimes think if we knew all, we should be more glad to get away.*** Robert Louis Stevenson, *The Strange Case of Dr. Jekyll and Mr. Hyde* (London: Longmans, Green, and Co., 1886), 57. According to his 1888 essay "A Chapter on Dreams," Stevenson drew inspiration, like Mary Shelley before him, from a dream.

208 ***Shhh . . . It's gonna be all right . . .*** Dialogue from the film *It's Alive*, directed by Larry Cohen (1974; Burbank, CA: Warner Home Video, 2004), DVD.

209 ***. . . rows of freaks . . .*** Doris Lessing, *The Fifth Child* (New York: Knopf, 1988), 81. Lessing wrote a sequel, *Ben, in the World*, which follows an eighteen-year-old Ben as he falls in love with a prostitute, gets caught up in a French drug smuggling ring, journeys to Brazil with a filmmaker, is kidnapped, imprisoned, and experimented on by scientists, and after escaping, determines he does not belong in the world and hurls himself off a cliff.

209 **There are only 350 cases of congenital radioulnar synostosis documented in medical journals.** Efe Okotcha, Matthew Goldfinger, Todd Bell, and Amanda Griffin, "A Rare Case of Congenital Radioulnar Synostosis," *Consultant* 62, no. 6 (2021): 8–10, https://www.consultant360.com /photoclinic/rare-case-congenital-radioulnar-synostosis. In browsing online forums dedicated to radioulnar synostosis, it is not uncommon to encounter people, particularly older individuals, who have never received an official diagnosis. Despite the lack of formally reported cases, there are undoubtedly many more people living with radioulnar synostosis worldwide. Boston Children's Hospital has treated thousands of patients with varying forms of radioulnar synostosis through its Hand and Orthopedic Upper Extremity Program. "Radioulnar Synostosis: Diagnosis & Treatments," Boston Children's Hospital, https://www .childrenshospital.org/conditions/radioulnar-synostosis.

VIII. Bigger Than Life

216 **. . . the last photograph taken of Richard.** *Close-up of Richard Jenne, the last child killed by the head nurse at the Kaufbeuren-Irsee euthanasia facility,* May 1945, photograph, National Archives and Records Administration, College Park, https://collections.ushmm.org/search/catalog /pa10049. Jenne, who was classified as a "feebleminded idiot," was murdered by Sister Mina Wörle, head nurse of the children's ward at Kaufbeuren-Irsee. She recorded the child's cause of death as "typhus." Wörle admitted to killing more than two hundred children via lethal injection and later received only eighteen months of imprisonment. Lynn H. Nichols, *Cruel World: The Children of Europe in the Nazi Web* (New York: Vintage Books, 2006), 3.

217 ***It is no shame to stand upon the scaffold.*** George J. Annas and Michael A. Grodin, eds., *The Nazi Doctors and the Nuremberg Code: Human Rights in Human Experimentation* (Oxford: Oxford University Press, 1995), 106. In addition to his role in the T4 program, Brandt was found guilty of coordinating and participating in myriad human experiments, which included tests on concentration camp inmates to study the effects of poison gas, freezing temperatures and high altitudes, malaria, typhus, jaundice, saltwater consumption, bone transplants, muscle and nerve regeneration, sterilization, and incendiary bombs.

217 ***I hope the exit is joyful—and I hope never to return.*** Frida Kahlo, *The Diary of Frida Kahlo: An Intimate Self-Portrait* (New York: Abrams, 2005), 285. The grandson of Diego Rivera, Juan Rafael Coronel Rivera, has speculated that Diego may have assisted Frida with her joyful exit, as a final act of love.

218 **. . . Last Supper.** Lubow, *Diane Arbus,* 679. According to Lubow, Arbus may have written more, as the final pages of her diary were later cut out by an unknown person, never to be recovered.